Teleworking
. . . in brief

T0300010

Mike Johnson

Routledge
Taylor & Francis Group

LONDON AND NEW YORK

First published by Butterworth-Heinemann

This edition published 2011 by Routledge
2 Park Square, Milton Park, Abingdon, Oxon OX14 4RN
711 Third Avenue, New York, NY 10017, USA

Routledge is an imprint of the Taylor & Francis Group, an informa business

British Library Cataloguing in Publication Data
A catalogue record for this book is available from the British
Library

Library of Congress Cataloguing in Publication Data
A catalogue record for this book is available from the Library of
Congress

ISBN 0 7506 2875 8

Composition by Scribe Design, Gillingham, Kent

Teleworking

. . . in brief

To JJ and JJ

Contents

Preface

It has been said that although Alexander Graham Bell invented the telephone, the real genius was the man who invented the second one, so that Alexander had someone to talk to! Perhaps that unknown person at the other end of the line could be described as the world's first teleworker. Whatever the truth, teleworking isn't new. Perhaps today, technology and the changes of the content of many of our jobs has allowed a lot more of us to sample the concept of teleworking at first hand, but it certainly isn't new. If you allow that a teleworker is anyone with access to a phone line, then thousands – possibly millions – of people have been teleworkers for years. It's just that no one has ever bothered to categorize them before.

I began teleworking over 30 years ago as a young journalist, when mobile communications meant a phone box and a portable, mechanical typewriter. In those days in western Scotland, keen young reporters could make more money reporting team line-ups, half-time and full-time action of local junior league soccer on a Saturday afternoon than the whole of your regular weekly pay-packet. For a brief period – at the age of 17 – I became the equivalent of today's teleworker supervisor. I managed to cover two matches each week, five miles apart, using two runners and a huge pile of pennies (four every time you made a call). The trick was – as today – to make sure you had unrestricted access to the technology (the pay-phone) to send the data (your brief report) to the remote server (then a usually male copy-taker who typed out your dictation). Just like teleworking today, imagination, dedication and hard work triumphed, I managed to successfully send copy to six newspapers in about 15 minutes – a triumph of modern communication – or so I thought then.

Sadly, many tradition-bound managers haven't moved much further than the basic phone in those intervening three decades. It might be portable, it might work on a beach at the Côte d'Azur, but that's about it.

Meanwhile, many of us in the communications business moved from mechanical typewriters to early PCs, remaining

Preface

only two or three steps away from the hobbyists and techies, evaluating what would help us and our often mobile existence. An early MacIntosh portable helped somewhat – even if the word portable was stretched somewhat beyond the size and weight limits of the dictionary definition – but it wasn't until more affordable lap-tops came that we were beginning to get somewhere. Then e-mail arrived. It meant we weren't just portable, we were reachable anywhere at anytime, with as much data as our lap-top could hold. We could run our businesses, do our work from anywhere.

This book was researched in Brussels, written in Scotland and edited in California. My daily outpourings were corrected by staff in my office and others around the globe, all for the cost of a local call. Hours later – or the following day – I could download their corrections and comments.

Telework provides all of us with access to a telephone line a whole new world to work in, to play in and to learn from. Thirty years ago, you dropped in your pennies and dialled your number and listened to those circuits clicking into place. Then you got an operator and you asked for 'the copy desk'. Then you dictated your story and hung up. We've come a long, long way since then.

Remember the TV show The Man From Uncle? When I was 12 years old I was deeply jealous of Napoleon Solo, not for his exciting life-style but because he had a phone that he could use from anywhere in the world, I coveted Star Trek Captain Kirk's 'communicator' as well. Now I've got my own and a whole lot more than that. Last year on the Star Ferry in Hong Kong Harbour I linked my GSM phone to a lap-top computer, dialled a local call access number and sent a message around the globe in seconds. I didn't need any money, I didn't need any wires, I didn't need to ask for anything or speak to anyone, not even Mr Solo or Captain Kirk could do that! We have indeed come a long way when we have surpassed 1960s science fiction in an affordable and user-friendly fashion.

Telework is what you make it, either as a tool for creating breakthrough strategies for your company or for creating a new working world for yourself. Whatever you plan to do, I hope that this book will help you in your quest and that telework will give as much pleasure to you as it has to me.

Mike Johnson
Largs, Ayrshire, Scotland 1996

Acknowledgements

It takes a lot of people to make a book like this work; without the professional input and support of telework specialists and enthusiasts in industry, consulting firms and academia it wouldn't have been possible. However, I would like to particularly acknowledge the very considerable help of BT for their much-appreciated support; Ian Culpin of DGXIII of the Commission of the European Communities for his initial enthusiasm and helpful contacts; the Finnish Industry of Labour; Gil Gordon Associates for much-appreciated support; Tony Hodgson for a thought-provoking set of scenarios; June Langhoff, author of The Telecommuter's Advisor; Jack Nilles for erudite ideas; Jenny Procter at AT&T in Brussels and Peter Wingrave at IBM in Portsmouth for their invaluable assistance. To all of them, and many others listed in the back of the book your help is most warmly appreciated.

Finally, I would like to make a special point of thanking my researcher for this project, Bodil Jones at Johnson & Associates. Without her hard work, enthusiasm, late nights and persuasive arguments on countless phone calls, faxes, letters and e-mails, this book would never have been written. More than anyone, she showed that teleworking really does work!

1

What is teleworking?

Despite the hype of recent years – culminating in the so-called 'discovery' of the Internet by private enterprise in the mid-1990s – teleworking is not new. Any sales representative serving a remote corner of any region or country, selling his or her wares and calling in the orders to a distant production facility, is – by most definitions – a teleworker. For decades, market research firms have used home-based tele-interviewers. Those infamous double-glazing, encyclopaedia and Bordeaux wine sellers are most likely to be home-based.

From the mass commercialization of the telephone in the 1950s, teleworking has been possible. The advent of the personal computer (PC) in the early 1980s gave added impetus to the idea and that was spurred on further by the Group Three fax machine, that gave fast, trouble-free performance at a price that became increasingly affordable. But it has only been with the easy access to cheap, high-speed modems, coupled to falling telephone charges in most countries (as well as price wars between international carriers), that the idea of a totally independent, stand-alone, yet instantly accessible worker has been a complete reality.

Add to those technical breakthroughs several other changes:

■ The flattening of hierarchies in most Western organizations, where advancement is more likely to be horizontal (what you contribute to the team or group) than the traditional vertical (seniority and tenure) model

■ The abandonment of the traditional job-for-life relationship between employer and employee to a more flexible form of employment where loyalty is expressed by the organization ensuring employability in the open marketplace

- The changes in the perception of work and the need and desire for a more rounded career/leisure life equation by an increasing number of people

- The need to reduce or eliminate commuting time, use of cars and public transport, particularly in urban environments where traffic pollution is at the top of local government agendas

- Corporate commitment to reducing overhead, from company cars to expensive real-estate

- The arrival of a new 'digital generation', whose values, lifestyle and 'keyboard' skills make them natural teleworkers and will create a definite boost for this type of work arrangement . . . and you have the complete ingredients – a recipe – for a massive work revolution.

in brief '. . .the single most anti-productive thing we do is to ship millions of workers back and forth across the landscape every morning and evening.'
– Alvin Toffler

Let's agree on what teleworking is

Today, there is only one barrier left for teleworking to overcome to be fully legitimized: getting everyone to agree on just what it is! Every book, manual, position paper and case study offers a different definition, and a different view. Others – in a need to be different – find a completely new name or phrase for the process of working away from a central office or group. These include: the electronic cottage, telecommuting, flexiplace and flexiwork, remote and distance work and networking. Add to that the fact that this growing industry's

observers and commentators have spent considerable effort in trying to categorize the different types of telework and the situation becomes even more confusing. What it comes down to is that one person's teleworking is another person's flexi-work.

Five myths of teleworking

Gil Gordon, regarded by many as one of the key players in promoting the telework/telecommute phenomenon and editor of the influential *Telecommuting Review*, warns anyone about to plunge into this great new world to steer clear of several dangerous myths that have grown up around the subject. Here's an adapted version of his Five Myths of Telecommuting, that should be required reading for anyone embarking on their electronic journey.

Myth Number One: Telecommuting is just for programmers or others using a computer terminal.
Fact Number One: It's a world for accountants, writers, analysts, sales people, research staff and many, many more. You are limited only by your imagination.
Myth Number Two: Telecommuting is just for parents who want to be at home with young children.
Fact Number Two: It's almost impossible to be a full-time telecommuter *and* a full-time parent. Also people of all ages and personal situations are candidates.
Myth Number Three: Telecommuting is a five-days-a-week deal, with no time in the office.
Fact Number Three: The time at the remote site can – and should – range from one to four days a week.
Myth Number Four: Telecommuting means working at home.
Fact Number Four: The home is only one possible workplace. Others include satellite offices, neighbourhood work centres, client's office and so on.
Myth Number Five: The biggest challenges in telecommuting are the technical ones.
Fact Number Five: With few exceptions, the technical aspects are relatively simple. The real challenges are with the human resources employed; selection, supervision, productivity.

Werner Korte, a director of Empirica, a communications consulting group in Bonn, Germany, who carried out a study on telework for the European Union, says that 'despite the fact that there was quite widespread consensus on what telework meant, a generally acceptable definition never existed and is still surprisingly elusive. In reality, people use the same terms to describe rather different things.' Those different things can take the form of the initial concept of the teleworker, as one who ploughs a very lonely electronic furrow in some cottage in the wilderness (insert your preferred country here), a salaried worker who spends one or two days a week working from home or another site outside the main company offices, or a group who get together in a telecottage, or local mini-service centre.

This is why the definitions get confusing, particularly that of telecommuting. That, according to most US experts and commentators – where the term 'telecommuting' first appeared – really covers workers who do not spend all their time at home, but have some physical access, one, two or three days a week to the organization.

Make sure that teleworkers have access to technical assistance either through a help-line or on-site visit if required. Downtime for a teleworker can be expensive for the organization.

In places like California – where Clean Air Acts and a need to get commuters off the roads is driving telework as a very serious alternative to traditional nine-to-five office life – telecommuting has been clearly defined as something different from just simple telework. For anyone seeking a definition like that, the Washington State Energy Office has come up with a very suitable – and widely accepted – definition of the telecommuter:

> A part-time work and transportation alternative that substitutes the normal work commute with the choice of working from home or at an office close to home. There are other, broader definitions, some of which include full-time work at home as a telecommuting option.

What seems most prevalent is that telecommuting is a US-coined term, while telework is the preferred, if broader term, used in Europe. Once again it isn't just the voltage of our PCs, faxes and modems that divides us !

4

chapter 1

What is teleworking?

Confused ? It gets worse than that. The problem is that telework has not only attracted definitions of how much time you spend doing it, but also where you do it, when you do it, what you actually do.

And in this lies the real problem of telework. Most definitions or categories of telework come up with just three areas (working at home, satellite offices and some type of neighbourhood work centre or telecottage), but, in reality, today's complex patterns of work need more than that to distinguish very varied work patterns.

The research firm Brameur in a study for the UK's Department of Transport helped to clear up much of the 'what do we call these people who work outside the central office environment?' question by suggesting that 'telework is where there is a clear change of travel pattern as a direct result of the switch to telework mode. Other forms of telework can have a TSS (Transport-Telecommunications Substitution) impact. For example a mobile worker, such as a salesman, a school inspector, or a field maintenance engineer, may switch from a pattern of attending a central office on most days prior to setting out on the travel part of the job, adopting instead a new pattern of going straight from home to the first customer call, thereby eliminating the home to work trip.' The report continues, 'Another form of telework is the relocation of entire work groups – for example when a company uses telework methods to concentrate its European customer services into a single country. A further example occurs when a local company subcontracts work formerly done on its own premises by its own staff to a company in another country, not only removing the commuter travel but also the work and the jobs from the local economy.'

Part of that, of course, is in a way good news. Rural economies – or at least those that recognize and can afford it – have a chance to begin to regenerate themselves, often creating a new alternative to farming and tourism, which until now have seemed the only viable economic activities. But this also means that the telework process and the ensuing revolution is going to pose lots of challenges on companies and institutions. To ignore it will certainly become impossible; to embrace it – like cuddling a cactus – requires careful preparation rather than blind enthusiasm.

Any organization – or individual for that matter – contemplating teleworking as part of their employment mix had better realize that as each day passes there are more and more complex permutations of what constitutes a telecommuter or teleworker. And when it comes to issues like promotions, compensation rewards and project allocations, you had better know who is doing what, or the whole concept of teleworking is not going to free your organization up but tie it down in ways that most of us have never imagined in our wildest corporate nightmares. Telework is not an idea, where one size fits all. It is something that needs to be tailored to your organization, your work patterns and, most important, your future strategy.

...and even more teleworking myths and misconceptions...

Managers considering telework as an option, or an idea whose time has come, need to look at the issues that it raises without prejudice. If you are considering the possibility of trying out a telework experiment, you have probably asked yourself many, or all, of these questions. Based on our research, the answers give a resounding 'yes' vote to some sort of telework scheme for many of our businesses.

Note: this list is also useful in developing an argument to sell the telework concept to senior management.

Myth Number One: There is no way to judge if teleworkers are *really* working – they could be taking the day off.

Not true! The employee's completed work or progress reports are the indicators that he or she is working. Managers of teleworkers should focus on the *quality, quantity* and *timeliness* of work and should manage by results rather than by observation. Also the manager and the employee should establish goals and objectives together.

Myth Number Two: Employees work less if they work unsupervised.

Wrong ! In fact, as opposed to working less, the reported tendency is for teleworkers to work much more. Employees who have demonstrated their commitment to work at the traditional office typically exhibit the same – or greater – level of commitment at the alternate worksite.

Myth Number Three: Social interaction cannot be maintained between telecommuters and their colleagues.

Think harder! In reality, there are many techniques for overcoming feelings of isolation. These include teleworking for only a portion of the work-week, core days in the office, regular communication by telephone, voice-mail or other media. In addition, teleworkers should be included in all scheduled meetings and office events and receive all staff notices.

Myth Number Four: I won't be able to reach teleworkers when I need them in a crisis.

Oh yes you will! In setting up telework arrangements, managers should agree and specify the hours that employees are available by phone, or require a check-in call at specific times during the day. As for being available in a crisis, how many office workers are sick, on vacation, travelling or with clients? The advantage of a teleworker is managers usually know where they are and can reach them by phone.

Myth Number Five: Our office culture is quite formal. Teleworking is too unstructured for such an environment.

That won't work either! Telecommuting may be flexible, but that does not mean it is unstructured. Always use a teleworking agreement to spell out exactly what you expect of an employee and agree on tasks to be performed and deadlines to be met.

Myth Number Six: Teleworking is a nice, simple solution for some of the work issues my organization faces.

Absolutely not! Telework is a tool that can help solve some organizational problems. But, for example, it should not be seen as a panacea for social difficulties, a solution to child care issues or as a dumping ground for non-performers.

Myth Number Seven: My employees should feel grateful to be able to participate in a telework programme.

Get real! Supervisors and managers often view telework as a favour they do for their employees, without any consideration or measurement of the benefits. In fact, telecommuting should not be seen as a perk or reward, but rather as one of the many human resource options. *Warning!* making it appear as a perk or reward may have a boomerang effect and create unnecessary resentment from former co-workers.

Based on material from the US Department of Transportation

Forget the hype and the hyperbole, telework is just that – working on the end of a line, whether with the most sophisticated equipment technology and money can provide or simply on the end of an analogue telephone.

So, let's lay the ghosts of the tele-something, tele-this or tele-that to rest. For the purposes of this book – this guide to where we can go – the term we are going to use throughout is teleworking. Reason? It covers everything under an acceptable umbrella. There is absolutely no use trying to identify and define different types of work and give them different names. Teleworking is already a reality; how it is managed, used and developed is the challenge that both the organization and the individual face. And while this book is primarily concerned with advice and ideas for organizations, it is important that both aspects – employer and employee – are taken into account. For it may well be that you will get the very best out of some of your employees if you free them up to work at their own pace in their own way. Equally you might, in fact, make the best use of your own time and talent as (even if you mentally don't refer to it as that) a teleworker for some part of your working period. Many organizations are already doing just that and their experiences tend to be on the positive side of the scale. While there may be those who take advantage, it would seem that for every one of those, there are nine others who bring more to their job in enthusiasm, productivity and new ideas.

The categories of teleworker

But it is important to work out what fits what kind of person and who they are and how they will function, if you and they opt for this sort of role. Chances are – whether you consider them teleworkers or not – you have some in your organization right now. Even you – if you stop and think – have already been a teleworker of some sort, however casual it may have been.

So, here's a quick introductory guide to who are the teleworkers of today;

8

The lone wolves

There are several genus of lone wolves, all with their own particular character and talents. Those of us approaching telework as a future concept for our organizations need to be very aware of the differences, because they are huge.

Lone wolf, type one: The home-alone worker. This is almost a mythical creature these days. Based on early experiments with teleworking, this was the employee who headed off to the wilderness and downloaded his or her daily tasks and uploaded them every evening. Largely confined to computer programmers and others of that ilk, there are few surviving today (at least in solo work mode). Early downsizing, said to be the cause of not being near the action and the politics, is the accepted wisdom for their demise.

Lone wolf, type two: The home-based worker. This group comprises thousands of employees who probably don't even consider themselves teleworkers. Sales representatives, insurance agents, service and repair staff, they don't sit at home all day, but they do have access and the use of the most sophisticated equipment, which makes them highly mobile and very cost-effective. They can ask for advice and assistance at the stroke of a computer key. This group are increasing their influence, reducing transport costs, office costs and getting closer to the customer than ever before. Organizations that have tried them like them a lot.

Lone wolf, type three A: The Electronic Road Warrior (ERW). Touted by some as the shape of things to come, ERWs are the twenty-first-century's answer to the travelling salesman. Often with an international brief and seldom in any office or home for long, they are armed with lap-tops, modem links, mini printers, GSM phones and every other gizmo. Highly specialized in their business and extremely effective in the right circumstances, they embrace the global marketplace with enthusiasm.

ometimes it seems veryone wants to ring our doorbell! Take a tip nd have a switch that vill easily disconnect it vhile you are working.

 choosing people for elework, it pays to look round the organization nd see who is already lone worker.
mployees who carry ut jobs with little iteraction or spend onsiderable time on a hone or working at a omputer screen are rime telework andidates.

Teleworking

Lone wolf, type three B: The Global Trader: increasingly what used to pass in many companies for a chief executive or marketing director. Often running the company at a distance (sometimes for a total of nine months a year) by e-mail and fax, they are forced to live on the road; to be where the customers are. Travelling constantly – and only going 'home' to clear the desk and smarten up the sales strategy – they are a new phenomenon that has yet to hit its peak. Effective when properly organized, they are highly intelligent and have created their own global social structure to compensate for their peripatetic life-style.

The groupies

There are three sorts of groupies in the teleworking galaxy, each with a slightly different approach to the way they relate to their organizations and each other.

Satellite groupies: These are self-contained mini-divisions of companies, that bring together a set of services (usually hardware and software) that can be used on a regular basis by teleworkers, whether they sometimes work at home or on the road. This enables both social interaction and an access to new developments, meeting facilities and so on that they otherwise would not have.

Neighbourhood groupies: Employees of different companies use a local centre, equipped and financed by several organizations, allowing them to share space and equipment facilities close to their homes.

Telecottage groupies: Mostly underwritten by funds from public authorities and local government, these are set up for use by independent freelance professionals – or company-employed lone wolves who need a social interaction – that give access to the latest IT equipment and meeting facilities that would not otherwise be available to them. They often provide training and development in IT-related subjects to facilitate use of telework in rural or industrially deprived communities.

in brief 'At the end of the last century, the Victorians were convinced that if traffic in London continued to increase, Piccadilly Circus would be several feet deep in horse droppings. This did not happen, because the car became more popular than ever imagined. Now we have the problem of the congestion caused by the car, and the more roads we build the more people use their cars. The solution is telecommunications – the problem is our lack of imagination. People have to comprehend the idea that the telephone wire is a motorway or railway down which you can travel in a split second.'
– Ashley Dobbs, president, Telecottages UK

The hot-desker

Increasingly found in the USA – where in some states legislation is fuelling the phenomenon – the hot-desker is spending one, two or three days working at home, then using the company's facilities to work face-to-face with co-workers, attend staff meetings and so on. Increasingly seen as both a social phenomenon, environmental benefit and motivational form of working, those of us in urban areas can expect this to become part of most of our working lives over the next decade.

The phenomenon of 'hotelling' or 'hot-desking' was initiated by accountants Ernst & Young in their Chicago office in 1992. Designed to meet the reduced office needs of employees who spend the majority of their workdays with clients, the firm makes available private workstations at a ratio of one to every two or three employees. A 'hotel' co-ordinator takes reservations for these workstations, assigning space, providing service and office support.

The offshore office facility

Usually established to take advantage of either cheaper labour or time zones, offshore facilities most commonly house back-office activity for insurance companies, airline reservation systems, customer help-desks and so forth. Their only link to the main facility is by technology.

Types of teleworkers

A study for the UK's Department of Transport suggests that there are three distinct types of teleworker:

1 **Marginal teleworkers:** who telework regularly enough (up to one day per week) to identify themselves with the term 'teleworker', but where the frequency or regularity is insufficient for telework to have become a routine aspect of the work pattern.
2 **Substantive teleworkers:** telework is sufficiently regular and frequent to have become a routine aspect of their work pattern. Those who work at home on one or more days each week.
3 **Dominant teleworkers:** telework is their primary mode or work. Those who work at home three or more days each week.

What this list illustrates is that virtually anyone can become a teleworker. With the investment in increasingly available and affordable technology, teams can operate independently, individuals can contribute to team thinking from a world away, senior managers can run their organizations while on the road.

What this has done is to speed up the redefinition of much of the work we do. For as technology allows us more spatial freedom – in that we don't have to go and sit behind a desk in department X on the twenty-seventh floor every day from Monday to Friday – we are able to spend more time actually working. The only limitation is the access to the technology. . . and just one other: the inability of many traditional nine-to-five managers and supervisors to accept what they see as a loss of control and authority.

But there is little those people can do to stop the chain of events that is now in motion. Increasingly people who face mind-deadening commutes are formally instituting an already informal, unspoken agreement. That they won't be coming to New York, London, Paris, Tokyo or any town or city near you every work-day.

The winners in this – both individually and organizationally – are those who have discovered the telework maxim, 'Work is something you do, not someplace you go,' or to put it another way, 'matching the job to the person, not the person to the job'.

Telework brings new possibilities and new needs together

Driven by the possibilities of new communication technologies undreamed of less than a decade ago, individual needs, organizational needs can now be put into another contractual relationship, without the need for either a constant presence or constant supervision.

A Rank Xerox guide to implementing telework illustrated the developments leading to teleworking as a viable option as the coming together of three separate areas that could now act as a single, powerful force, easily harnessed for the betterment of both the collective company and the individual worker (Figure 1.1).

People
- Self-regulation
- Build personal competencies
- Portfolio 'employable' lifestyle

Organization
- Need for flexibility
- Reduce overhead costs
- Focus on core activities

Figure 1.1

Technology
- Increasing capability
- Falling real costs
- Great ease of use

Office Worker	Teleworker
Reasons for commuting to an office	*Alternative workstyle*
Imposes time structure	Sets time limit on tasks
Meets people outside the nuclear family	Fewer contacts = more to talk about regular meetings at office and contact with office via phone
Alternative source of identity and reassurance	New career structure being created
Defines personal status and identity	Personal status can improve as a result of the work flexibility to make decisions and how work is organized
Offers scope to utilize experience, knowledge and talents	Shorter, more explicit tasks, utilizing the individual's personal talents
Drives motivation from others	Inwardly directed and self-motivated
Is a source of reassurance and personal contact – need to fit in and appear committed	Security based on output and relevance of contribution

This is where the real revolution comes: the ability to align technology with the wants, needs and expectations of both employer and employee in a link-up that was never possible – at least to this extent – before.

Examining that fundamental change, that breakthrough, in our ability to better manage, communicate, control, and measure distance workers, Rank Xerox suggest the following differences that help our understanding of telework's possibilities and how they could apply to our own organizations.

Clearly for those with the correct strength of character and self-motivation – not forgetting the ability to 'work' the central office and stay fully appraised of developments – telework can have considerable advantages. The upshot of that also has implications for how we tackle work at the most basic level. For, as telework begins to take over many of the old-fashioned office tasks, it is going to be vital to focus on creating self-reliance and break away from the old ways of teaching people 'how to apply for jobs'.

Telework IS the new world of work in action

As work patterns – already shifting in terms of guaranteed employment for life to a new contract of employability – change, we are going to have to educate those in salaried employment how to stay employable – how to know who will give them the best training and the best tools to be marketable when they are no longer required. In this teleworkers are going to feature with increasing regularity and – for those with particular specialization – increasing success, whatever present employers might say to the contrary. For in the new world of work, which virtually all of us in Western economies are coming to accept, telework not only makes sense but also widens the job opportunities dramatically. It also creates a whole new spectrum of work which literally encompasses the whole world.

Management Technology Associates (MTA), a UK-based consulting firm, in a report on the economic and employment implications of telework, concluded that telework had the following positive impacts on a local, national or regional economy:

- Firms that successfully adopt telework gain significant benefits, particularly in productivity improvements and cost reduction – making them more competitive
- In a global, networked economy, this increases local prosperity and generates work opportunities
- Local firms can adopt the techniques of telework and teletrade to reach out and provide services to distant

customers, thereby bringing wealth and work opportunities to a local economy
- If local authorities, economic developers and business support organizations understand the principles of telework they can create an environment and develop workforce skills that are attractive to inward investment in the new networked economy (for example, by becoming a desirable location for concentrative telework projects).

But MTA also identified several negative aspects of the telework equation:

- Work that is loosened up by the introduction of telework methods can just as easily be teleworked away as it can be teleworked in
- Companies that are slow to adopt telework mechanisms and – above all – the underlying techniques of open electronic networking, will be very vulnerable to the penetration of their local markets by competitors who embrace these methods
- Telework enables employers to recruit more widely and to place the work where they find the best combination of skills, costs and motivation. Towns, countries and regions that don't gear up to embrace the networked economy can find even local employers moving work away.

Most significantly, MTA relate the present job revolution to telework: something most other studies have ignored. Their scenario bears serious consideration, not least because it is already happening. 'As with any technological change, the development of the networked economy is accompanied by a wide take-out in old-style jobs and lots of confusion about where new jobs will come from.' Here are some of MTA's conclusions:

- Telework increases the fragility of old-style paid employment
- A very high proportion of telework opportunities arise in the self-employment mode rather than as paid employment in steady jobs
- Companies will increasingly seek to have greater flexibility by having few permanent staff and having as much work as possible done by flexibly employed staff or under contract

16

- Permanent posts will have a shorter life-span. The idea of a thirty-year career with one employer is already a thing of the past
- Telework, teletrade and open electronic networking present immense economic and work opportunities, but few of these opportunities will be in old-style companies doing old-style things. The new environment calls for individuals to be more inventive and creative in their approach to business and work.

Getting employers and employees over the fear barrier

As in other aspects of changing work patterns it would seem that those who cannot – or won't – adapt are going to be the big losers. And that goes for both corporations who won't try out teleworking, because they think they will lose control of their people, to individuals who need that, so-called, water-cooler camaraderie that the traditional office brings.

All the same, figures speak for themselves. Studies in the USA report that over three-quarters of current teleworkers say they are more productive than they were: certainly a figure no employer can afford to ignore. Additionally, teleworkers cite less stress, reduced transportation costs and more control of their work as other advantages.

However, many would-be teleworkers are shying away from asking if they can sell the car and stay at home. A survey by US-based Telecommute America! concluded that, 'despite the potential of this alternative work-style to produce more and better work, 61 percent of would-be teleworkers have never even asked their employers permission to telecommute. Most of those polled, who said they wanted to telecommute, were afraid to ask, fearing their managers would view them as less than serious or committed workers. They believed their employer might not support such a work-style and were reluctant to ask, especially in a downsizing and merger environment.'

But under both economic, social and government pressures this reluctance and hesitation looks set to change – fast. Therefore, the message for those that want to stay ahead is, get out there and at least experiment – as quickly as you can – or get left behind in the slow lane.

As psychologist Jane Firbank, who carried out a study for BT, the UK-based telecommunications firm reported, 'In the past, some managers have been reluctant to have their staff working from home because they saw it as a threat to their authority and control, but companies are now embracing teleworking because they can see the benefits.' Firbank adds, 'Properly managed, new technology can enhance the quality of life not just in hours saved in commuting but by enlarging their social networks and increasing their job satisfaction. Commuters are concerned that they will miss the office atmosphere and will find it lonely at home, but these drawbacks are outweighed by the personal benefits of flexible working.'

All the same, companies need to understand that not all employees are suited to a sudden introduction to telework. Many people just don't adapt to working part of the time on their own – they need the security blanket that going to an office brings (see Chapter 6). Those who fear isolation, are easily distracted and have little self-discipline are not likely candidates for telework. Equally, those who get paranoid out of missing what's going on back at the office, or feel they will be losing out to advancements and promotions, need either special treatment or not being put on the telework list at all.

Most of all, it is important for companies to realize that teleworking isn't taking your staff and sending them home to work forever. It is a rational way to increase their productivity and your own, reducing costs for them and the organization. But it is also understanding that they do need to come together not just by e-mail, fax or phone, but physically, whatever the work location, at least on some sort of regular, pre-agreed basis. Organizations with two- and three-day teleworkers are finding that the combination seems to work well at least in the initial stages.

There are a thousand-and-one distractions just laying in wait for the less than committed teleworker. One gave the excuse he couldn't work, because the birds in the tree outside were singing too loudly!

What seems to be most typical is that companies begin the process by experimentation – pilot trials that involve a small department or a percentage of a division. Based on those experiences, a final telework strategy can be worked out that meets the needs of the organization as it begins to take the concept further into the organization as a whole. However, be warned: many companies are reporting the problem that once the experiment is over, employees don't want to go back to that five-day-a-week commute – ever!

18

Employers also need to realize that teleworking – or some form of it – is not going to be an option or a choice. Rising costs of real estate, regulations on commuting, environmental considerations, access to distant markets and manpower, changing needs of skilled workers and external competition will force us to take this route and make teleworkers – permanent or part-time – out of all but a small core of key managers. And even they will be on the road for much of the time, teleworking for much of their professional lives. While some might fight it – fearing that loss of control – others have already embraced it. And it isn't just an American fad that might go away if we ignore it.

Pro's and con's

A study of 500 full-time workers by the research firm Gallup UK for communications company BT listed the top five reasons for teleworking for individuals and organizations – it also listed the concerns.

Individual benefits
- Flexibility
- Increased convenience
- Saves travel time
- Reduces commuting
- More efficient working

Individual disadvantages
- Distractions
- Need for self-discipline
- Need for special equipment
- Lack of social contact
- Insufficient space

Company benefits
- Saves office space
- Increased productivity
- Staff goodwill
- Savings on relocation costs
- Retaining staff

Company disadvantages
- Need for face-to-face
- Prefer traditional methods
- Setting-up costs
- Communication problems

Perhaps the power of these new technologies to change the way we work is best put by Andersen Consulting, whose ground-breaking office in Paris has 1150 employees but can accommodate only 600 at any given time, the others are on the road, working, selling or just 'home-alone', catching up with the bits and bytes of their electronic mobile world.

Teleworking

The networked company demands new-style leaders. An executive who participates in the company's e-mail and discussion forums can take the high ground in corporate communication – and it will do their image a lot of good as well.

Estimating that they are saving in the region of US$1 million annually their managing partner for Western Europe, David Andrews, enthuses, 'Historically business strategy has always driven technology. Now you see technology driving and enabling business strategy – that is a fascinating new trend.'

With a world that is changing faster and faster each day, with the traditional job-for-life relationships between employer and employee becoming obsolete, technology is already enabling businesses to map out new strategy. It's not a case of why should we do it, but when can we get started. The rest of this book is about just that: practical insights into getting you and your organization into the telework era.

Executive Summary

- ■ Telework is one way – and only one of many ways – to meet the challenges of a new world of work.

- ■ Telework will be boosted by the wants, needs and capabilities of the new digital generation just entering full-time work.

- ■ Telework is seen as a way for rural communities to attract new business and play in the big business world.

- ■ Telework splits into different work categories. It's important to define where you or your organization fit in.

- ■ Telework today is a product of the marriage of latest technology tied to emerging organizational and individual needs.

- ■ Telework isn't a job for loners any longer. Often it is just one or two days a week, carried out in a group, or involves intensive and frequent voice and data communication.

- ■ Telework will force people to think employability, not tenure; to focus on self-reliance, not organizational coddling.

- ■ Telework is not for old-style companies doing old-style things.

2 What can teleworking do and where is it going?

Teleworking is here to stay. It may not be for everybody or even every organization, but for the majority of us, failure to explore the advantages of having some employees or contract staff working at least partly from home or other locations would be a big mistake.

Few experts who have studied the development of teleworking think that it will ever go beyond 25 per cent of full-time staff. However, with full-time staff, a breed that is slowly vanishing through downsizing, mergers and natural attrition, we can expect that all of us are going to see the teleworker as a significant part of our operations in the years to come.

But there are three key drivers of teleworking that need to be examined before any organization can embark on developing any sort of viable strategy. These three not only need to be considered, they need to be in some sort of overall harmony if any telework solutions are going to work.

First, there are strong external forces beginning to impact on the way we work: traffic congestion, urban pollution, strikes and natural disasters. Add to that the availability and sinking cost of sophisticated communications equipment that makes staying in touch an ongoing, easy option. Second, there are strong internal forces, rising costs of employment, the need to attract qualified staff, the repositioning of many staff workers in other locations, the cost of maintaining office space. Third, there is the way many people want to work.

Teleworking

Flexibility is the keynote here. Many well-paid, highly qualified people just don't want to commute four hours each day to an office. Equally, many of them are on the road for much of the time anyway.

'What' is more important than 'where'

A report by UK communications giant BT puts many of these points into perspective, saying, 'In the future, what people produce will matter more than where they produce it. From the organizational viewpoint, that means an all-round acceptance of new working practices, top quality communications and more flexible employment contracts.' The BT report goes on to suggest that anyone trying to make a case for teleworking in the organization shouldn't try to list all the benefits it could bring. 'The best way of justifying it is to pick just one benefit and use that as the main driver,' they say.

Here are five examples from BT of how a change in the mode of work can add to bottom-line results:

Taking the hassle out of selling

A telesales call-centre has the hassle of having agents on standby every day. Paging or calling them every time they are needed is inefficient. Worse still, as calls are going unanswered at busy times sales are being sacrificed. This organization justified teleworking on the basis that they could better manage the peaks and valleys of the business by bringing additional agents on-line much faster (increasing overall sales) and also needing fewer staff during slack periods (lowering the wage bill).

Enhancing customer service

An organization that trades internationally across time zones is using enhanced customer service as their main network driver. They reasoned that given instant access to data and other information their senior sales consultants will be able to provide a better and more personal service from home than from a bustling office environment.

Saving space and saving money

Another organization realized that the sales force's desks were hardly used. So they calculated the cost of the space and used that as the main driver to move to teleworking.

Thinking big in small business

A systems manager in a small company was supporting four regional offices and spent most of his time travelling between them all. With modern communications and systems the same manager now works from home, and can add to his responsibilities as the organization develops.

Retaining talent

Most companies spend a lot of time recruiting people and developing them. Then, due to sudden changes in people's circumstances, they can lose that investment. By having a more flexible approach to working, there are opportunities to keep your talent on the team through teleworking – even to the point of enhancing it.

But there are other developments we need to consider, to fully understand just where telework and its other flexible working alternatives can fit into the changing workplace, at the same time guarding against what could – and sometimes can, go wrong.

Not just pushing buttons

According to Tele Danmark Consult, in a report prepared for the Commission of the European Communities in 1996, there are two competing circles of influence using advanced communications to enhance our work options: we had better know where our organizations stand on all of this if we are to throw ourselves into telework either as a promoter of the concept or a 'let's see how it works' guinea-pig.

Looking at the downside, co-author of the report, Jeremy Millard, says 'It is clear that we need to move away from the vicious downward spiral of much previous use of information technology and advanced communications. This was based upon job rationalization and an emphasis on process automation, efficiency and speeding up operations, in situations where labour was de-skilled and alienated.' Adds Millard's co-author, Chris Jensen-Butler, 'The worst images in such a scenario – which are real enough for many – leave people to simply push buttons on machines, in a revisit to the Chaplinesque Modern Times nightmare.' He goes on, 'Instead, we need to move towards a virtuous upward spiral, in which advanced communications is used to transform business processes, contribute positively to business, market and service innovation. Where labour growth and empowerment are essential components, because human capital is firmly locked into the creative and competitive processes. This scenario recognizes that social cohesion and security are necessary prerequisites to such processes, as well as to labour flexibility.'

The vicious and virtuous circles

Millard and Jensen-Butler explain the vicious circle as one 'where competitiveness is built upon reducing labour costs and attempt to speed up existing processes and make them more efficient by using stand-alone information technology. The overriding concern is with cutting the cost of labour, short-termism and downsizing. The alternative scenario is the virtuous circle, 'where human capital becomes fully locked into creating competitiveness, so any cuts in labour costs no longer become a sensible option, but where other cost savings can be achieved by making the production process more efficient. For example, by using advanced telecommunications to reduce coordination and transaction costs, achieving economies of scope and by making long-term efforts to develop future business and markets.' Just what the technologically-driven, networked and organized teleworker is able to do.

Let's look again at the coming together of technical, organizational and individual change and possibility. Millard and Jensen Butler's view is supported by many, if only organizations had the wit and wisdom to recognize that there

What can teleworking do and where is it going?

is a revolution taking place – one that benefits business and the individual in a win–win equation. If you need to ask 'what can the technology do, and – more important – what can the people linked to that technology, do for me?' look no further than the list below.

From	To
Technology	
■ Information technology used for automation of existing processes and activities by making them more efficient and speeding them up	■ Use of information technology and advanced communications to integrate geographically separate activities, resulting in an intensification of overall activity, as well as the creation of completely new types of work processes, activities and market opportunities
Interorganizational	
■ Vertical production links and production processes	■ More horizontal economic networks (e.g. outsourcing to small specialized firms, outworkers and sub-contractors)
■ Islands of information technology in each organization as inward-looking technology	■ Networks of organizations integrated through advanced communications, as outward-looking technology
■ Simple trading relations between fixed-role suppliers and customers, with competitors and other players excluded	■ Complex trading relations in which organizations can simultaneously be competitors, suppliers, customers and distributors
Organizational	
■ Hierarchical, bureaucratic organizations	■ Delayered, networked organizations
■ Large, stable organizations	■ Down-sized, smaller, ever-changing configurations (e.g. virtual enterprises)
■ Internal decision making to control and coordinate activity	■ External market signals drive and coordinate activity
Work patterns	
■ Single and fixed task demarcation	■ Multi and flexi-tasking (a reversal of the traditional division of labour)
■ Central, hierarchical reporting relationships	■ Decentralized, horizontal and integrative relationships
■ Static, geographically concentrated work patterns	■ More mobile, distributed work patterns (e.g. teleworking and direct service getting closer to the customer)
Individual	
■ Life-long, full-time, fixed job skills	■ Changing, flexi-time, multi-skilled jobs
■ Once-and-for-all education	■ Continuous education
■ Jobs for life	■ Evolving jobs and work portfolios

Source: TeleDanmark Consult, 'Employment trends related to the use of advanced communications', June 1995

This list of where we are moving from and where we are going to in our patterns of everyday work makes the job of the teleworker more acceptable with every passing day.

Telework is far from a full-time concept

One thing any of us contemplating taking the plunge into telework as part of our business must consider is that most of the people involved don't work from home full-time. Average days a week out of the office seem to be around two to three, which – when you stop and consider it – is something that lots of us do naturally anyway. Depending on our job description, many workers travel as a matter of course and have always done so. All teleworking does is formalize – in many cases – existing working arrangements.

Also, don't forget that systems engineers, technical installation specialists and others can spend large slices of their annual work in another company. Add to that the increasing number of 'implant' staff, who are either on contract to work in another company or provide a service to another organization (travel agencies, catering groups, auditors all do this on a temporary or permanent basis) and it is easy to see that telework is not a new phenomenon at all.

The newness, the reason for all this excitement about teleworking, is the ease of access to the new teleworker's main tool, the electronic interface – that either wasn't there before or was unaffordable. Today the cheapness of PCs and their required peripherals – and the ability to tie them into user-friendly, secure networks – has tipped the balance increasingly in favour of the teleworker, making them almost as much of a key player to the organization as someone who occupies a corner office in headquarters. And with the advent of cheap, practical PC-compatible video links, staying home-alone will soon be a thing of the past.

Of course, nothing will ever replace the touch and feel and atmosphere of being face to face in a room with people, but that also has to be an intrinsic part of the teleworker recipe. This is not banishing workers to the ends of the earth, this is giving them time to do things better. And studies around the world all point to one thing: teleworkers thrive on the experience.

John Bakke, a consultant with Telenor Research and Development in Norway, comments 'Teleworkers thrive. The majority report a low level of stress when comparing with

26

"ordinary work" and they report few problems in concentrating while working from home.' Bakke adds, 'Concerns that teleworkers would become detached and isolated were unfounded as they felt a belonging to their "other" workplace.'

But Norwegian teleworking experience – approximately 10 per cent of the population fit into this category – has highlighted one issue: the need to talk to the people they work with. Although many use sophisticated communications systems to receive and send work, using the telephone has proved to be the number-one communications method. E-mail may be all very well and the fax a welcome tool, but picking up the hand-set and talking it over with a supervisor or a colleague on a project still has the advantage. This is why predictions of an increase in the numbers of teleworkers when video links become common are easy to accept.

Employers cite the advantages

But before that day dawns on us, reasons for creating a cadre of teleworkers are often different depending on the business being done. However, a study by telecommunications firm AT&T in 1995, based on a poll of 200 senior managers in Fortune 1000 companies, provide – from a US viewpoint at least – what employers saw as the key advantages of telework:

Better employee morale	79%
Reduced costs of office space	64%
Aids the retention of valuable employees	63%
Reduced stress among employees	63%
Reduced absenteeism	61%
Increased worker productivity	58%
Encourages workers to take initiative and make decisions on their own	48%
Improved customer service	33%
Reduced costs of equipment	27%

So, as can be seen, experience of users shows that morale, productivity and retention rates go up, stress, absenteeism and office costs go down.

But the survey also reported on what those same senior managers perceived as the disadvantages a company might have to deal with when using teleworkers:

Reduced control and supervision by manager	63%
Harming of team concept	63%
Jealousy of non-teleworkers	54%
Added costs of equipment	49%
Added costs of telecommunication services	48%
Used to meet child care and other domestic needs	29%
Reduces worker productivity	20%
Reduced timeliness of work completion	17%

Loss of control and worries about team effectiveness and morale are very much at the top of the list of most managers' fears and concerns when confronting teleworking as a concept. And with more and more organizational emphasis on teams and task forces, potential champions of the teleworking concept can find their ideas and plans overruled by worried senior executives. The survey picked that up, with 64 per cent of those polled saying that 'they were not convinced the advantages outweighed the disadvantages' and 64 per cent admitting to 'difficulty in overcoming traditional managerial attitudes'.

Suffice to say, experiments with a few key personnel can do little harm and are possibly the only way to demonstrate to dyed-in-the-wool managers that there is another way to work. Indeed organizations with teleworking teams operating at a distance from each other – but coming together for prearranged meetings – report excellent results in both morale and productivity. This is borne out by the attitude of those 200 senior managers to what they saw as the employees' attitudes. The top three responses were: better morale (80%), an increased feeling of empowerment (71%) and a better balance between work and family life (70%).

In the UK the Warwickshire Rural Enterprise Network (WREN) has experienced the same concerns as that of their US colleagues. According to WREN's observations the biggest force against telework is 'the need for tighter management practices'. This is particularly true in a period when most businesses are under pressure. This and 'the need for teamwork, data security concerns and the social isolation of some teleworkers' are the top disadvantages they experience.

Another issue that WREN raise – and one that is beginning to be an issue wherever telework is on the increase – are concerns about 'health and safety, confusion over tax status, social benefits, employment rights, and other new working from home issues'. But they feel that these three pressures of internal and external needs and the needs and expectations of the individual will eventually bring the vote down in favour of teleworkers. WREN cite 'potential productivity gains of up to 45 per cent' as a carrot that few companies can resist to at least experiment with telework. They also believe that 'demographic changes – bringing pressure on employees to retain valued staff and on employees other pressures to adopt flexible work patterns (e.g. to care for ageing dependants)' will be sure-fire drivers of this revolution.

Who can telework?

Knowing the types of personnel who can switch to teleworking (covered in detail in Chapter 5) is vital to the success of any experiment or trial. Here are a few basic criteria to look out for:

- Self-motivated, responsible and reliable
- Able to work independently with little supervision, but knows when to communicate and ask for things
- Results oriented, capable of setting own priorities and deadlines and meeting them
- Successful and secure in their present position
- Understands the organization and appreciates its culture
- Highly adaptable to changing work requirements
- Excited and enthusiastic about teleworking

The downside is that in many cases these are the people you would rather keep inside the organization. But chances are if you don't let them try it they will ultimately telework for someone else. This is where the proverb a bird in the hand is definitely equal to two in the bush!

As another BT report points out, 'you and your job were made for teleworking' and they go on to say that specialists, managers, clerical staff and what they term 'nomads' are all super-suited to this form of earning a living. According to BT, 'there are four main job areas acknowledged to be most suitable for teleworking:

1　Specialists, by the very nature of their work, often have to spend a large percentage of their time working independently. If you're a technical writer, computer programmer, data analyst, designer, engineer or consultant, as long as people can contact you, the chances are that you can become a teleworker.
2　Managers often prefer to telework two or three days a week. Away from the office you can really concentrate on producing reports, preparing presentations or writing reviews. Then return to the office to share your ideas and implement your plans.
3　Clerical staff can save themselves time commuting and their company the money spent on office overheads. If you carry out data-entry work or telesales, why are you waiting on a railway platform?
4　Nomads spend most of their working day behind a wheel, visiting various sites or meeting clients. With quality mobile communications, if you're a salesman, you can significantly cut the time you need to spend checking on who's called for you. Better communications will also improve relations between yourself and head office and with your customers.

Telework: many forms and characteristics

Other definitions of different types and sub-species of teleworkers abound. Management Technology Associates (MTA) provide some useful pointers to defining different types of workers in today's complex work environment.

As MTA says, 'The term telework is often interpreted by the media and people generally to mean "home-based'. But this is misleading, telework can have many forms and characteristics.'

Home-based teleworkers

Working at home, instead of commuting to an office, this applies to: employed teleworkers, where the individual's contract of employment includes the home as a place of work as well as – or instead of – the employer's premises; self-employed or freelance teleworkers, where the individual chooses or prefers to work at home. Generally, these self-employed people will 'follow the market' – if the employer wants them on-site, they'll work on-site.

Ten tasks for teleworkers

As we keep stressing, teleworkers aren't permanently home-based personnel – most commute two or three days and stay at home the rest of the time. This gives the best of both worlds: time to think and time to act. If you plan work well,  this means that you can hold meetings and other people-intensive work during your time in the office and do the other jobs at home.

Here are ten top tasks for teleworking time:

1 Creating, writing and editing reports and proposals
2 Preparing budgets
3 Maintaining personal databases
4 Preparing and developing contracts
5 Developing sales and business plans
6 Finalizing staff reviews and bonus plans
7 Thinking, reading and reflecting
8 Catching up with business correspondence
9 Project management and task force assignment planning
10 Desk research by phone, fax and e-mail

Too often, all of us have to try to squeeze these tasks in between constant interruption by superiors, subordinates and colleagues. A few days a week teleworking from home would give you a better grasp and understanding of the business than if you were at the office five days a week.

Informal – or even illicit – teleworkers

The individual and his or her immediate management see the benefits of teleworking and adopt the practice, but with no corporate approval and sometimes flying in the face of corporate policies that are opposed to teleworking. Currently there is some evidence that indicates informal teleworking is more prevalent than formal supported programmes.

Entrepreneurial teleworkers

It has always been common for people starting a business for the first time to work from home until they can afford the overheads of a so-called 'proper' office. Now an increasing proportion of first-time entrepreneurs have the confidence to reject the idea of a formal office and continue to grow their businesses on a network basis, with all the staff working as best suits them as individuals.

All of us should remember that categories of workers and what they do are becoming increasingly blurred these days. Trying to pigeon-hole people is not a useful exercise when you are trying to get them to think outside the restrictions of the organizational box that they live and work in: to empower them to work much more on their own initiative. If all the superlatives of what teleworking can do fall on their face, one thing will endure: it makes people think differently about not just who they are but how they do their job.

Thinking about telework as an alternative is not a bad thing, either for the employer who wants to examine new work ideas and keep his key staff, who perhaps have other ideas for a future lifestyle that don't embrace a four-hour commute each day, or for individuals who want to be on the winning side – job-wise – as the work revolution speeds up. Because be sure there are going to be winners and losers as the move toward a more virtual – if not completely virtuous – workplace gains both impetus and credibility. It won't be long before the days of 'going to work' will, quite possibly, be regarded with disdain by many. The man or woman with the gainful, secure, future-related occupation will be those that only leave the house to see a client or to attend the occasional face-to-face get-together.

32

Be aware of the losers as well as the winners

According to recent research in both Europe and the USA here are the losers and the winners:

The losers

- Lower-skilled workers are in decline, largely due to a reduced demand for their services brought about by competition from low-wage countries. Also lack of retraining and an inability to access new skills make them less likely to be re-employed.
- Any type of manual or clerical worker whose organization has not given them access to new technologies. A surprising number of clerical workers remain computer illiterate.
- Workers who are unable or unwilling to adopt new work patterns and skills.

The winners

- Professional and information workers.
- Workers involved in creating, structuring and managing information.
- Workers who are able to add a 'human touch' to customer contact as a value-added response (remote, teleworkers staffing customer hot-lines are a good example).
- Unskilled or semi-skilled workers who do have computer skills.

At the organizational level technology and the way it can be applied is also changing the roles of the business architecture. Professional roles (specialists in many cases) are becoming interchangeable with management; middle management are switching to team and project leaders and case workers, rather than assignors and assessors of work carried out; secretaries are becoming facilitators and organizers (often of work teams and not individuals).

As TeleDanmark Consult's Jeremy Millard and Chris Jensen Butler point out, 'these changes are not being driven by just advanced communications'. Indeed not, the technology is just enabling companies to finally achieve many things they have wanted for a long time. Only now they are dealing with the art of the possible. In that recognition of new ways to work, telework is a major and attractive possibility.

in brief 'Innovative technology and creative applications are erasing traditional workplace boundaries and enhancing people's lives at home, at work and on the go.'
– Bob Allen, Chairman, AT&T

Telecommuters are germ free

So keen are telecommunications giant BT's marketing staff at highlighting the virtues of telework they get perilously close to oversell at times. Here's their take on the healthy aspects of telework. '...working from home cuts out or reduces commuting induced stress. So you start work relaxed when others are already stressed and when your working day ends you still have time for leisure, while others still face an unpleasant journey. Also, by avoiding travelling and working in crowded environments, you're no longer exposed to other people's germs.'

Much of the reason for this is based on an ability for the teleworker to be a very flexible and multi-talented supplier to the company. Although not simply confined to teleworkers, the expectations of today's corporations fit that category like a glove. As Millard and Jensen Butler report, tasks and people are also being affected by the introduction of advanced telecommunications. Tasks are moving from:

- Single to multi-tasking
- Simple to complex tasks
- Repetitive to flexible, creative tasks
- Support to direct tasks (e.g. customer contact)
- Physically tiring and boring to intellectually and psychologically demanding.

Supporting those changes are the way people are developing to meet these needs (or could it be the other way around, with the people who want to do it helping to drive the technological, organizational, individual equation?) from:

- Specialist to generalist/specialist (workers are now expected to undertake a range of tasks at both low and high level, technical (vertical) as well as horizontal (organizational).
- Low to high job enrichment and satisfaction (as recessions free more and more people to move out of protective jobs, watch this indicator climb very fast indeed!).
- Less to more stress and isolation. A lot of work is required to counteract some of the negatives that are going to build up in teleworker and other work-at-a-distance employees.
- Single to multi-skills: computer, personal and business skills (all in the one same package).
- One-time to continuous training (much of which is the employee's responsibility to demand and act on).

The TeleDanmark Consult report summarizes 'Overall, people need to be able to take the initiative themselves within what is becoming, simultaneously, a richer and more varied work environment – as well as a more stressful and unstable one. This can, in the right circumstances, produce greater job enrichment and work challenge.' As long as they can get some kind of work-guarantees a lot of people are going to be seeking that enrichment and challenge through the medium of telework, either permanent or just a few days a week.

Powerful reasons for teleworking's popularity

This balance of needs between those of the corporation and those of the individual looking to get away from the commute–work–commute treadmill will be one of the main reasons for the continued development of telework. A report by the Arizona Department of Administration, Travel Reduction Program, forecasts that '10 per cent of the country's adult civilian workforce will be teleworking by the year 2000'. They add that there will be some powerful reasons for the popularity of this relatively new work arrangement:

- The rapid development of technology that allows fast and easy movement of information
- Increasing concern with the environmental, social and personal costs of commuting
- The desire of organizations to recruit and retain the best employees possible
- The pressure on organizations to improve the bottom line, but doing more work and getting better results with fewer resources
- Employees find it more difficult to balance their work and home lives as the number of two-working-parent and single-parent households rises
- Employers and employees alike are under pressure to improve work quality and productivity.

A similar report from Oregon's Department of Energy (note that these are both US states with relatively low population density and they are already doing something about this!) lists organization, community and employee benefits like this:

Organization benefits

- ■ Teleworking can result in better job performance
- ■ There is improved employee morale and job satisfaction
- ■ It's a good way to retain valued employees and recruit top-quality new people
- ■ It provides access to persons with disabilities, part-time and semi-retired workers and workers who live in remote areas
- ■ With fewer people in offices, less office and parking space is required
- ■ The use of teleworking shows that an organization cares about the community and the environment
- ■ There is less sick leave and absenteeism among teleworkers
- ■ It can save money in the areas of hiring, training, health-care, office and parking space.

Community benefits

- ■ It helps decrease traffic congestion
- ■ It conserves limited energy resources because of low gasoline consumption
- ■ It helps make the air cleaner
- ■ It offers greater employment opportunities for disabled, part-time and semi-retired people and residents of rural communities.

Employee benefits

- ■ Employees have the opportunity to be more creative, more productive and do higher-quality work
- ■ They feel better about themselves and their jobs because of the trust shown in them and the responsibility and independence given them
- ■ They gain flexibility and greater control of their work schedules and their lives
- ■ They save time and money and experience less stress because they don't commute as often.

The successful telecommuter

Telecom Made Easy author June Langhoff says that a successful telecommuter is a disciplined self-starter who likes to work solo. Take this survey to measure your chances – or those you want to telework – for success (the more check marks, the higher your score).

1   Are you well organized and goal oriented? At the very least, you'll want to brush up on time-management skills.
2   Are you effective at controlling distractions? Family, neighbours, and pets will compete for your attention.
3   Do you work well with a minimum of supervision?
4   Are the social aspects of the office environment relatively unimportant to you?
5   Are you an effective communicator? You'll need to be. Most of your interaction will take place over the phone or via e-mail.
6   Can you set aside an area of your home to be used exclusively as an office?
7   Are you comfortable with the idea of working solo?
8   Can you get along without office support systems and personnel? (No more copier, message-takers, typing pools. No PC-guru or network administrator at your beck and call.)
9   Can you easily get along without in-office reference material (or arrange to get copies for home)?

Reprinted with permission from June Langhoff, author of *Telecom Made Easy*

Europe and the telework revolution

In Europe, the European Commission – often slow to get its act together, particularly in anything involving high technology – has been actively pursuing a teleworking policy for some years. The Commission says that it has a mission to 'promote teleworking in homes and satellite offices so that commuters no longer need to travel long distances to work. From there they can connect electronically to whatever professional environment they need, irrespective of the system in use.' By the end of 1995, the Commission had created twenty pilot teleworking schemes in European cities involving around 20 000 workers. Their aim is to create or help create 10 million teleworking jobs by the year 2000 – just three years away. Although they agree with others on many of the advantages of teleworking, the European Commission see five distinct areas that are worth noting:

1   Boosting local employment: responding to the aspirations of 96 per cent of Europeans to find jobs in their own regions
2   Cutting business costs: making use of available skills and eliminating the need for large, central offices, located in expensive and congested urban centres
3   Creating more flexible working hours: especially in part-time jobs, addressing the needs of both employees and employers
4   Saving energy and reducing pollution: cutting down on commuter travel and easing traffic congestion in cities. It could in this way save more energy than any improvement in energy supply infrastructures or other energy-efficiency measures
5   Giving individuals greater responsibility and flexibility: allowing work and other commitments to be better matched and increasing the quality of life.

These are fine words, and there seems little reason to doubt the sincerity of EU officials, who have seen the writing on the wall for the traditional concept of jobs for life over many years (it is hammered home to them every day in the continued astronomically high unemployment statistics), but while a collective EU may espouse lofty intentions, a quick peek under the mother of Europe's skirts shows that among the petticoats of sixteen member states there are a few rips and rends that will take an army of lawyers years to fix.

Non-Europeans, bored with the dubious delights of Euro-harmony, may feel it appropriate to stop reading here. But be warned before you do that; anyone contemplating setting up a teleworking operation, either as an organization or as an individual, had better dust down the corporate counsel or your legal representative and find out just where you stand. Conflicting laws across borders are one thing, misunderstandings and misinterpretations on a national level are par for the course as well.

According to a European Commission report on telework that examined the legal aspects in Belgium, Denmark, France, Germany, Italy, Portugal and the UK, 'no law specifically forbids telework. However, the legal and regulatory environment or certain practices in most countries do little to permit the development of telework.' It goes on, 'No specific legislation covers telework and the homeworker status does not exist in several countries. Teleworkers run the risk of not being able to enjoy the rights usually accorded to workers and even of finding themselves in a precarious situation.'

How the unions view telework

In addition to hinting that Europe's trade unions don't look upon telework with a great deal of favour, with the comment that 'the creation of telework could be regarded as a means for employers to evade their responsibilities and reduce costs' the report calls for a lot more work to try to formalize some EU-wide understanding and legal notion of what telework really is. Cross-border teleworking, for example, is a hotch-potch of confusion, depending on who does the hiring, who does the work and which national state of the EU each one is resident in at the time.

It should also be said that in that great free market of the United States, trade unions also cast a suspicious eye on the development of teleworking: even the CWA (The Communications Workers of America), that represents 600 000 journalists, printers and telecom workers, is watchful of developments. A spokesperson for their union, mindful that employers could use telework assignments to reduce or obliterate permanent employee contracts, has suggested that employers often choose to ignore items like increased heating and lighting bills and peripheral equipment costs.

Back in the EU, the position on taxation is equally confusing, and also of concern to the EU. The Constraints on Transborder Telework report states 'Telework is characterized by new conditions of work, where the worker is not anymore under direct controls. It becomes easier to have some activities without declaring them and which tax

40

authorities might have lots of difficulties to identify. Consequently, telework creates new types of risks of tax evasion.' The report adds, 'The problem is further increased by the fact that certain teleworkers may work on a part-time basis or in precarious situations, and may then be tempted to have other activities than the ones which they declare. Moreover, telework may give birth to a new generation of "technological cheats" whom it will be necessary to guard against.'

No wonder the unions don't like it. They can see telework as a cheap and easy way to get around their collective agreements with employers. No wonder the EU doesn't like it, they cannot control it right now. Individual states don't like it either, suspecting – rightly in a lot of cases – that the advent of cheap fast, instant cross-border data transfer is open to considerable abuses, of which not declaring what you are working on is just one. When you add in the protection against invasion of privacy, who pays what tax, custom controls, value-added tax and what does and does not constitute a business, you are left wondering whether telework is really worth it.

But if the EU is worried, that is strong evidence that private enterprise and private individuals are not. Thousands of companies are operating national or transnational telework schemes. If they don't they will be losing out to competitors. As long as the legal costs don't get to ridiculous proportions they seem to feel it is a necessary and profitable investment.

Also, the EU – as with other regional organizations – doesn't have much choice but to accept what is already a de facto way for many to earn their living. Faced with an unemployment level that hovers around 12 per cent on average, and won't go away, they are not in much of a position to stand in the way of technological progress. If they do, teleworkers can move to another location in Europe (non-EU Norway and Switzerland are handy if they'll let you in) or even to another continent.

The EU report appears to be aware of how foolish it could quickly look if something isn't made to happen soon. It also echoes concerns that if the right sort of sensible legislation isn't in place soon, the EU could be one of the big losers in both jobs and high-technology workers. 'Whatever the country or field of activity,' concludes the report, 'telework,

t's important to specify *ll* the issues that might *b*ecome points of *c*ontention in telework *a*greements. For *e*xample, the creation of *a* work location at home *d*oes not make a regular *c*ommute to the *t*raditional workplace a *b*usiness trip.

as in all new forms of work, is currently in a state of legal limbo unprecedented in other areas of employment.' It adds 'One must keep in mind that this may act as a formidable disincentive to embark on a telework programme, specially for the smaller firm [where EU job growth is coming from]. It takes as much time and cost to address and resolve the numerous inevitable issues for three teleworkers as it does for 3000. It is thus the quest for greater flexibility that must guide the legal innovations that are indispensable to the development of telework.' Not to mention the economic development of the EU.

Remember the adage? with telework, the work goes to the worker, they don't have to turn up to get it. They can – and frequently are – anywhere they want to work from, not where people would want them to be.

However, considering telework and the increased flexibility it offers, there are several other areas that bear looking at in the development of this form of work, especially in how organizations, busily reinventing themselves, can win big – not in grabbing hold of the hearts and minds of employees who want to work differently, but in harnessing those needs into a truly flexible business structure that saves money and is more in keeping with the fast-moving times we now live in.

New strategies to keep workers

While many executives worry about lack of control – less team spirit and a break-up of the organizational culture – and individuals rave about their newly empowered, less stressful status, there is another – potentially bigger – issue at stake in the teleworker trend. One that properly handled can give hard-pressed companies a useful competitive advantage. Faced with the inevitability of teleworking and the need to keep those top performers tied however umbilically to the body corporate, new strategies must be invented – not new strategies that weaken an organization but new ideas and concepts that strengthen it.

Consider this: a company, a division or a department that has been built around flexible working standards is flame-proof. Needs may come and needs may go, projects can

42

begin and end and the organization is built not only to accept this but to make the most use of the flexible approach to doing business. People can come and go, telework, meet for a few days or a few weeks if required and then disperse again. Equally, telework faced up to with enthusiasm and proper organization has even greater cost benefits. People in a telework environment can be switched to new tasks involving new people without costly moving expenses or work disruptions. Work in high labour cost areas can be transferred to remote sites, where high-level skills are available at a fraction of the cost. Finally, teleworkers have one other advantage to recommend them. They don't waste time getting to work during transport strikes, snowstorms, protest marches, presidential visits and the daily traffic jam. They are up and working. As long as there is a plan – a workable, practical, flexible plan – teleworkers can save money and give an organization a new set of ammunition to develop new products and services, improve customer satisfaction and allow fast changes in overall direction.

At the personal level, of course, the critical point in all this, is that it is the smartest of employees who will see the advantages. Better organized, more confident and more productive than their counterparts, it is they who will be leading the charge for greater independence and a greater say in how and when they commute to the real office in town. This, of course, is one of the real issues for the future of teleworking as a viable concept; it isn't the steady plodder who will be the first to recognize the potential inherent in teleworking but the over-achiever.

But in all this euphoria there is also a darker side that needs to be discussed as part of the overall debate. For every top performer who might just say au revoir if you refuse him or her the chance to telework at least some of the time, there are the others who, already insecure in their nine-to-five job, would look on working at a distance as a trip to purgatory. Additionally, unscrupulous employers could well use teleworking as a method of changing the employee contract. That's one of the reasons trade unions in Europe are eyeing this newly devised work method with some suspicion.

Let's face it. If the world of work is changing and there is a new invisible contract between employer and employee

The economics of teleworking

The financial case for one company
A major financial institution's pilot teleworking scheme
(20 senior managers teleworking and 4 secretaries relocated)

Costs per annum	Prior (none) £	Teleworking £	Difference £
Exceptional costs of change amortized over five years:			
New equipment £3550 × 20	71 000	71 000	
Manager's time × £35 70 hours	2450	2450	
Estimated loss of production time × £35			
(20 people × 8 days × 8 hours)	44 800	44 800	
External course/consultants' fees	1000	1000	
Less: retaining trained personnel	−50 000	−50 000	
	Box total £69 250/5 years = £−13 850		
Office space			
Rent	86 400	–	+86 400
Rates	21 600	–	+21 600
Secretarial support/space	–	–	–
Electricity/air conditioning/heating	12 872	3000	+9872
Building maintenance	2160	–	+2160
Garage/parking spaces/fees	–	–	–
Building insurance & security	10 080	4000	+6080
Washrooms/leisure facilities	2496	–	+2496
Time lost/sick building syndrome	13 440	–	+13 440
Clothing allowances	300	–	+300
Commuting			
Cars (capital per annum)	–	–	–
Running costs	18 894	3750	+15 144
Train/bus fares adjust.			
± London waiting	86 400	72 000	+14 400
Time lost/disruption/sickness			
Epidemic	11 200	–	+11 200
Operating			
Teleworkers' salaries/fees	–	–	–
Secretarial salaries	56 000	28 000	+28 000
	(London rates)	(Local rates)	
Managers (of teleworkers)	131 600	171 080	−39 480
£35 p.h. minimum	(3760 hours)	(4888 hours)	(1128 hours)
Gossip time with colleagues and			
secretaries	164 500	–	+164 500
Equipment, furniture and machines	See new equipment above		
Telecoms: rent/buy phones	See new equipment above		
Productivity up by 11% on average per manager			
Hours worked	1410 hours	1565 hours	155 hours
£35 p.h. per teleworker × 20 people	887 000	1 095 500	108 500
Total savings per annum	£444 412		
Less exceptional costs per annum (box total)	£13 850		
Total savings	£430 562		
Total savings per teleworker	£21 528		

Source: BT, UK

that doesn't offer a job for life but a chance of getting another job – and nothing more than that – then telework is going to be a precarious route for many. Full-time workers today could find themselves part-time or contract workers – with little or no tenure – tomorrow. While entrepreneurs, start-ups, specialists and confident contract workers will embrace it wholeheartedly, others will find it a noose that ultimately tightens around their necks. Still more, possibly well suited to the teleworker mode, will find that domestic arrangements just don't work out and they have to find a few other souls of a similar persuasion to get their tele-bungalow off the ground. Being at home all day is not always what people imagine, especially couples who have learned – and quite possibly like – being apart for much of the working week. The phrase 'I married you for life, but not for lunch' springs readily to mind.

Overshadowing all of this is the Internet revolution. So far most forecasters have been wrong in assessing its mushrooming growth. But one thing is certain, it makes working at a distance, even a world away (as we will see in Chapter 3) a practical reality. Hopefully many of today's workers, already struggling with their keyboards, will be able to understand the next technological breakthrough and find some way to accommodate it in their lives.

Are you really a teleworker already?

On the other side of the coin there are those who are unabashed teleworkers and don't know it. Recent surveys show that many senior managers, especially those being headhunted or recruited into new jobs, won't necessarily relocate to the 'new' city. Preferring to stay where they are as far as house and home is concerned, and well aware that much of their job is based on travelling for much of the time, they drop by the office when the air schedule permits, but otherwise head home on Friday and climb aboard another jet on Monday morning. These jet-set workers are the ultimate teleworker. Equally comfortable in their seldom-visited office, hotel room, first-class cabin, client's conference room or the office over the converted stables, they are a new and rapidly increasing breed that chief executives everywhere have to build into their recruitment and retention strategies.

Additionally, the new generation – the digital hordes – weaned not on TV but Nintendo are beginning to appear in the workplace, in flat organizations it won't take them long to bob like champagne corks to the top. To many of this generation – born with a keyboard as an extension of their fingertips and a Pentium chip for a bolt-on extra brain – telework won't be a novelty work idea but their first experience. What they will make of it and what electronics will aid them in doing remains to be seen. Suffice to say that organizations that want to be competitive are going to have to create whole new methods of work and reward if they want to attract the best and the brightest.

in brief
'The new mobile technologies, including lap-top computers and wireless communications, allow us to work anywhere and at anytime. This new equipment is sure to cause a revolution in the workplace.'
– Rich Malloy, editor-in-chief, *Mobile Office* **magazine**

With a good deal of cynicism already manifesting itself, the advice to many bosses has to be that you need to find as many ways to create some semblance of loyalty and trust as you possibly can – or suffer the consequences. Whether high-flyer or capable performer, the intelligentsia of our corporations are beginning to opt for some new-age work patterns. Telework might not be an option, it might be the only route you can take.

Executive summary

- Telework is unlikely to ever represent more than a quarter of most company payrolls and not more than 10 per cent of a country's workers (but don't bet on it!).

- Telework is gaining ground fast thanks to new technology that makes it both practical and manageable as never before.

- Telework can help managers retain people on payroll who don't – or can't – commute any more.

- Telework has been proven to save significantly on office rentals.

- Telework at present is a new winner's circle for professionals and highly qualified specialists.

- Telework has positive affects on employee morale, studies report.

- Telework plans should not be a cause of concern for managers who fear a loss of control – results show productivity and contactability actually improve.

- Telework can create a fireproof, totally flexible organization that can switch to new challenges and opportunities at a moment's notice.

- Telework lacks a lot of legislation. Care should be taken in setting up distance-work-sites by both individuals and organizations.

- Telework is not for everyone. Many people don't want it and wouldn't be any good at it anyway.

- Telework is prevalent in every organization in some form or another. When you're not in the office, chances are you do some kind of telework. How many others in your organization already do?

3 Who teleworks and why?

Asking the question 'who does it and why?' might be the wrong way to go about looking at telework in the latter years of the twentieth century. Today, it is more like, 'who isn't doing it and why?' because there is increasing overwhelming evidence that organizations and individuals are turning to this form of work, either out of preference or necessity. With powerful technology that has been around for years in one form or another now at last totally user-friendly, teleworking for at least some of the working week is set to take off.

Of course, many – if not most – telework arrangements are ad hoc: a supervisor agreeing to let someone take work home, a travelling executive locked away in a hotel room writing proposals and creating budgets. But one thing that these ad hoc – seemingly accidental – arrangements have in common is that, except in a few cases of abuse, they continue over time. Reason? Both parties, employer and employee, realize that they are a productive way to get work done. They are especially productive where complex pieces of work – long reports, financial plans, strategy papers – need both time and peace and quiet to do them properly. Everyone who has ever worked in an office must have asked their boss at some time or another a version of 'can I take this home and work on it in peace, please?'

Keeping the customer mystified

One company that is on the cutting edge of teleworking technology is Shiva Corporation – named after the many-armed Hindu god. Their local area network rover (LanRover), allows employees and other outworkers to hook up wherever they are, no matter what systems they are using. Often customers never need to know that they are on-line with a teleworker.

■ Baxter Healthcare have several employees teleworking part of the time, using a pool of lap-tops as the hardware. Teleworker, Richelle DiCola reports, 'I train employees on how to use our software and they don't even know, I'm not in the office.'

■ Output Technologies in Kansas City provides printing and direct mail services to clients, using workers and freelancers in different states. Through the Shiva interface, creative types rarely come to the office. Comments systems manager Bill Hudson, 'Our artist in Denver can dial into our graphics group, transmit a file with a revised illustration, print the illustration in our office, and hold a conference call with us and our clients, while we all have a copy in our hands.'

■ Marine Spill Responses, a Washington-based oil-spill clean-up group, uses the Shiva's remote access technology to connect members of clean-up teams at regional command centres, faraway spill sites and even ships at sea.

These are examples of teleworkers, who can be a real-time part of any organizational discussion or debate, giving full value but from a remote site.

Never forget that not everyone wants to telework. Examples abound of workers who live close to their place of work who gain from the social interaction and have no commuting problems. Furthermore, they see their future prospects tied to being in the right place at the right time – and to them that's head office. Alienating these employees can have a counter-effect to productivity gains from teleworkers unless properly managed.

Sometimes formalizing these casual arrangements changes the way people look at this form of working. Formalizing it, calling people teleworkers, having policies, procedures and productivity measurement guidelines can seem to many a step that they don't want to take. Others, happy with their nine-to-five social cocoon, have a fear of what they consider a new form of work that they are certain won't suit them.

Telework has entered a new, organized phase

But it's not new, it's just a lot easier than it used to be. But like all ideas whose time has come, the users up to now are going to have to accept that – just like the 'discovery' of the Internet by big business – so telework has entered a new, organized, regulated phase.

in brief

'As the births of living creatures at first are ill-shapen, so are all innovations, which are the births of time.'
– Francis Bacon

This organized phase, with companies actively pursuing telework opportunities mainly to cut costs or speed up operations also means that the nature of telework has changed as well. Often it isn't working from home, or even a remote tele-centre. More and more it is a large group of employees at a purpose-built location. Thus American Airlines organizes customer service and ticketing for large parts of the world from Barbados; computer programming for the London Underground is carried out by a firm in India; American insurance companies use sites in Ireland and north-east England to speed up insurance claims (using the time difference to advantage as well as the hourly wage differences); other airlines use Turkey and Asian countries for ticketing and customer service. Technically termed concentrative teleworking, other examples are computer maker Dell and American Express, who have brought together customer support centres for much of Europe to a concentrated centre in Ireland.

However, to the predictors of huge job losses in countries with high wage rates it needs to be pointed out that it is only to low-wage countries that have the right infrastructure, available technology and a skilled citizenry that telework will migrate. Currently, aside from a few examples in central cities in Asia and the West Indies, there is little challenge – and little likelihood of it – from other developing areas without a massive injection of capital and resources.

Managing the messages

Stories and cases abound of bosses who have given up the daily commute and gone virtually virtual. The problem is that you cannot turn all those calls and e-mails into thin air. Those that have done it, and claim that anything is better than sitting in a city in an over air-conditioned or overheated office cubicle, say there are a few rules to follow:

■ Scrupulously download and respond to your e-mail first thing and archive the key messages. Don't get upset if you get 100-plus messages a day, research shows that most managers get over twice that in face-to-face discussions in meetings, phone calls and drop-ins to the office.
■ If you have staff out there in cyberspace do three things:

   1 'Meet' them on conference calls at least twice a week, even if it's just to say 'Hi'. Don't wait until there's a crisis or a favour you need.
   2 Schedule 'physical' meetings with all your staff at least twice a year. The money you save on real-estate bills should more than cover getting people together – and meet with others on a regular agreed schedule.
   3 Make sure you know and agree a teleworker's core time when they absolutely, positively have to be there and they know yours. Equally, make sure that you respect their down-time and they do the same.

Indeed, it would seem that anything is possible. Just what is being done, and what can be done was never better illus-trated than in an article in Flexible Working magazine in 1995. In a listing of companies with 'well-known teleworking schemes', Flexible Working profiled eight diverse businesses and highlighted why they did it and what the success factors were. What it shows is that there are many applications for telework and a lot more still to be created. This is their report:

- **Rank Xerox**: Cutting overhead costs, particularly office costs, was an important aspect of Rank Xerox's networking scheme. As a result of the project, up to 60 per cent improvement in productivity was reported. In addition, Rank Xerox has converted executives to teleworking on a self-employed, guaranteed work basis. Not only has this reduced central offices, it has lowered large contingent costs such as redundancy and pensions for executives and has decreased the number of head office staff required to service the senior people.
- **Allied Dunbar**: A top-ten life assurance company, Allied Dunbar has been built up over the last 20 years almost entirely by home-based sales people, with a minimal head-office core team.
- **Prudential Assurance**: Employs over 13 000 people, with approximately half of them home based. Supported by local offices, where home-based teleworkers are unlikely to have their own desk.
- **Computer Programming Associates**: A division of ICL with a teleworking team in excess of 300, reporting consistently good results.
- **Infopress**: A public relations and communications company, Infopress looked at teleworking to fulfil two objectives. First, they wanted to maximize the efficiency of their media evaluators whose job is to determine whether PR campaigns are reaching target audiences and they felt that unbiased judgements are best made away from office distractions. Now all their media evaluators are able to work where they are most efficient – at home. Inforpress also wanted to increase the productivity of their PR professionals, and as much of their work demanded uninterrupted concentration, they found that this was best achieved at home. They report an increase in productivity of 50 per cent.
- **American Express Travel Services**: Their Houston, Texas, office reported recently that their sales people who work from home achieve US$30 000 more sales per annum, handle 26 per cent more calls and are 46 per cent more effective.

- **Lombard North Central**: This financial services group reported that they were saving over £5000 per year in direct costs per teleworker and experiencing between 10 and 20 per cent productivity increase.
- **BT**: They installed ten of their directory enquiry operators at their homes. Staff were less stressed (this is a cost saving in terms of money spent on stress management and stress-relief programmes). Staff also took less sick leave (again a cost saving) and were also more productive.

Elsewhere, banks, finance houses, retailers and service organizations are seeing the value of telework both in savings and in increased motivation and productivity. As David Brain of Systems Synthesis and Andrew Page of Protocol Communications report, 'In the largest sense, teleworking is a term that simply draws attention to the way most of us now work. Increasingly in our daily routines we use the telephone, answering machine, fax, networked computers and advanced telecommunication services such as voice mail, audio and video conferencing, call diversion, mobile telephony and so on to provide our skills at a distance from the places at which they are applied. We do this in collaboration with colleagues, sub-contractors and customers who are widely dispersed. Moreover, the progression to teleworking will be especially accelerated as telephone numbers are routinely assigned to people rather than places.' Brain and Page add, 'The key factor in the way we can telework is location dependence. Teleworkers are those people that have appreciated that they don't have to be tied to fixed locations. The workplace is becoming less important than the work process.'

Telework is part of new management practice

But why all this new interest from corporations, eager to carve a few more percentage points out of people's performance? Brain and Page suggest that 'the present recession has forced companies to re-examine every aspect of their business. Teleworking can be seen within the context of new management practices and general efforts to increase the effectiveness of company operations.'

Current examples of this are the computer company Unisys, where call diverting has hit new heights of efficiency and where a seamless system allows consultants and sales people to respond by phone or keyboard without the customer knowing exactly where they are. Accountants Coopers & Lybrand claim to have saved 20 per cent of their head-office space, with a similar system that now works for more than 2000 of their people.

Brain and Page continue: 'Increasingly, essential company information is held on computer databases, which can be accessed from virtually anywhere with a phone line. Today, successful companies are defined more by the capabilities and robustness of their computer and telecommunications networks and less by the size and prestige of their corporate headquarters.' Brain and Page add a challenge to management as well: 'teleworking both requires and encourages a shift in management practice towards management by results, focusing on output, rather than wasteful adherence to bureaucratic procedures. Good tele-managers, manage work, not people.'

Getting virtual to survive

One of the main trends that is making the so-called virtual organization head towards popular reality is the plain fact that many professionals, although touted as the big winners of the telework revolution, are in danger of losing out to nationals of other countries, where work can be done cheaper: the new market economies of Eastern Europe with a high proportion of well-trained, numerate professionals are a case in point.

Michael Wolff, a Scottish-based business process consultant, reckons that the creation of a virtual network – in this case for engineering design – will not only ensure the livelihood of Western European professionals but will also cut project costs at the same time. Comments Wolff, 'increasing use and convergence of information technologies have presented both opportunities and increased global competitive pressure on engineering design operations'.

His solution is to get a group of engineers together in a network and pool resources and skills based on the reasoning that by creating a virtual organization:

- Individuals can market their services in a global marketplace and create higher-quality work and lifestyles without reducing standards of living and without having to move to where work is originated.
- The cost structure of a distributed virtual organization is substantially lower than that of a conventional organization. The virtual team has low office and support costs and individual contractors can charge less as they work from a home base.

According to Wolff, 'the combined benefits that arise from re-engineering the process and distributing a significant portion to home-based resources in high-cost areas enables projects organized in this manner to compete favourably with those that are currently being outsourced to low-cost offshore centres.'

This is a classic case of how Western professionals can be self-sufficient, gainfully employed and competitive at the same time by using telework to eliminate the overheads that would otherwise render these types of jobs obsolete in the longer term.

A prime example of good tele-management practice, Brain and Page note, is IBM, 'where IBM people increasingly carry a powerful smart-card, rather than waste space in fancy, dedicated offices. With their smartcard, an IBM person can tap into essential company data – from service manuals to contact lists – wherever they are. IBM offices accommodate people on a desk-sharing basis. People locate themselves where they can be most effective.' Indeed they do! IBM – whose acronym once stood for 'I've Been Moved' – has changed much from its centralized management days. Now one of their key recovery imperatives is what they call Network-Centric Computing (NCC). The idea is that not everyone wants to work in the same way and, according to IBM's plan, 'NCC gives you choice and freedom – when and where to work. Not everyone's choice will be the same, and unlike the past you will now have the opportunity to plan the workstyle that suits your lifestyle best.'

Following major restructuring, IBM's operations routinely cross borders as a matter or course, 'our colleagues may well be in other countries, no longer necessarily in neighbouring towns and cities', they say. 'Open business is our business today and open places of work are more relevant to our way of work and are in fact imperative to our success. In such an environment it becomes increasingly irrelevant to create local business boundaries and protected areas.' IBM adds, 'High walls, big divisions of space, closed doors and hidden rooms are relevant to a past culture not that of today'.

To achieve this, IBM have created three levels of meeting and working space, in addition to working from home or on the road: hubs, satellites and drop-in locations:

1   **Hub locations** are the major business gathering places, with a range of facilities that reflect the size and the catchment area of customers. Hub locations also provide 'touch-down' facilities for mobile personnel.
2   **Satellite locations** carry less common facilities and feed from the hub locations for a number of their requirements (e.g. stationery).
3   **Drop-in locations** are a microcosm of business life, but they provide all the essential services required to do business. They allow IBM to be in the communities they need to serve, but in a compact manner.

With flexibility a paramount need, project teams a key resource and cross-department interaction vital, IBM's new work strategy makes sense. It even specifies that it doesn't want people locked away, but sharing work areas and meeting places.

Here's how IBM describe services and work patterns at the central hub:

As the centres of many businesses, identifiable team bases are encouraged. At these centres will be the support staff (normally assigned specific workplaces given their static work patterns), surrounded with all their team paraphernalia; awards, achievements, wins, party notices, photos and so on. Gathered round the team base will be a rank of workplaces with different characteristics to be used on a need basis, as and when by the mobile personnel of the team. All this space is a common resource for the use of everyone and is therefore not assigned to any one person on the team. These places should be thought of as company resources on short-term loan.

While each business will probably have an identifiable base, the boundaries between businesses will not be defined. This is to encourage synergy and use of common resources. It also allows businesses to expand and contract (and their neighbours) without the attached high costs of reconfiguration.

Enabling the disabled

Virtually all altruistic and enthusiastic promoters of telework have at one time or another made the same assumption: 'Telework is a wonderful way for disabled people to enjoy gainful employment. Working from home they will feel a part of the business and the community.' Sadly, the assumption has proved to be, for the most part, wrong.

Reason? The last thing most disabled people want to do is stay at home. So the successful pilot schemes in countries like Finland, Greece, Ireland, Italy and Scotland have concentrated on getting disabled workers trained and equipped in tele-centres, where they have the social interaction that they need as well as work.

Often, these tele-centres lack much marketing muscle to get their name and services known in their region. However as the European Union estimates that over 70 per cent of disabled people can use PCs and other communications-related equipment 'without any special adaptation', it is definitely a way to create a legitimate, fully paid job for these people in tomorrow's society.

As Jane Berry of the Warwickshire Rural Enterprise Network in the UK says, 'the integration of training with a friendly and well-resourced workplace means that people who are disadvantaged can more easily bridge the gap between training and work, returning to use for profit the computers that they trained on in a familiar environment. Freelancing in a supportive environment which provides IT help, business leads, work contracts and a social dimension can help those traditionally marginalized from the labour market to build the confidence and create the experience they need.'

Advice to employers is: find out what exists in your region.

Rooms for meetings are given priority to customers and visitors. However, they are bookable for IBM internal use, on the proviso that customers will take priority, even at short notice. Increasingly, however, people are finding the coffee and restaurant areas make hospitable as well as useful discussion space away from some of the interruptions of the workplace (both from and to colleagues). Here's how IBM see the facilities:

Hubs	Satellites	Drop-in
Shared workplaces	Shared workplaces	Shared workplaces
Some workrooms	Some workrooms	Some workrooms
Central meeting rooms	A few meeting rooms	A meeting room
Central print/copy	Local print/copy	Shared workplaces
Restaurant	Snack bar	Some workrooms
Banks? Travel?	Records storage	A meeting room
Records storage	Some customer meeting	A print/copy area
Marketing centres	facilities	Real coffee area
Customer meeting facilities		
Support to satellites & drop-in locations		

Not only in Europe is IBM having successes with its style of Network-Centric Computing approach, they recently concertinaed 400 000 square feet of office space into a 100 000 square-foot facility in New Jersey. Indeed IBM's mobile strategy programme involved its managers as strategic partners in the highly successful and rapid conversion of most of its US marketing and service workforce to fully mobile status. IBM has reported that costs on real estate have been reduced by US$35 million in one year.

A smaller, but nonetheless equally innovative solution to changing workstyles came from the advertising firm Chiat/Day. They gave every employee a portable phone and a lap-top. Now when an employee wants to come to the office for a day, they get their cabinet on wheels that holds their personal files. Andersen Consulting have done the same in their Paris offices, saving space and commuting time as well as upping productivity.

The most popular item is a mobile storage cabinet by Herman Miller called a 'Puppy'. It's a secure file drawer on wheels that is stored in a common area called 'the kennel'. In the morning you take your puppy from the work area, take out the picture of the wife and kids, computer disks, files and whatever else you need. – *Facilities Design & Management* magazine.

Back in the USA, Natalie Fay of the Bay Area Telecommuting Assistance Project in Oakland, California, reports that 'firms as diverse as Deloitte & Touche, 3Com, Hewlett-Packard, Regis McKenna and Pacific Bell found significant increases in productivity from their own teleworking programmes'. She goes on to illustrate other prime uses of teleworkers to improve organizational bottom-lines either in savings or productivity, or both:

in brief.

'We are a society overwhelmed by pollution, traffic jams, and seemingly endless commutes to work. Time with our families is often minimal. And so we look to teleworking as one solution to these formidable problems.'
– United States Office of Personnel Management

- Spar/Burgoyne, a firm that checks prices and shelf space at supermarkets and drugstores, was facing high absenteeism and employee turnover rates among workers who key-in data for analysis. By allowing the employees to work from home the firm retained employees and increased efficiency.
- Amex Life Assurance has had a telework programme in place for more than five years, with 20 telecommuters – mostly underwriters – who work at home one or two days per week. The company did not supply

computers or other equipment and was able to implement the programme at zero cost. They report that they have had no employee turnover among the teleworkers in the last three years; highly unusual in the life assurance field.

■ American Express Travel Related Services (TRS) faced declining productivity among its workforce. Although they maintained a network of 50 satellite offices around the country TRS discovered that these were becoming increasingly obsolete in terms of assistance to the sales representatives, concluding they would be much more efficient working from home. TRS provided a comprehensive support package for its representatives, including lap-top, printer, fax, copier, two phone lines, car phone and reimbursement for all business expenses. They also threw in a one-time home-office set-up allowance of US$1000. However, TRS made it clear to the sales people that 75–80 per cent of the work-week was to be spent with customers and prospects and less than 15 per cent at home. Numbers of calls per day increased by an astounding 40 per cent; customer satisfaction ratings went up by 28 per cent and employee satisfaction rose by 25 per cent.

Virtual offices save dollars and make sense too

US experience shows that creating telework centres to support homeworkers adds value to home-based teleworking. As more employees from the same organization telework either from home or a local telecentre, the company can begin to redesign its main offices for less permanent use and generate serious savings. Estimates show that it costs between US$10 000 and 15 000 annually (including rentals, equipment, maintenance) to keep an office space open for an employee.

More and more companies, more and more gains

Elsewhere, more and more companies are reporting gains from a well-run telework programme, either for gingering up bored office workers or getting sales and service people to hit new highs in orders and satisfaction levels.

Julie Dodd-Thomas of Pacific Bell's teleworking programme in San Juan Capistrano in California says 'we actually started our teleworking programme back in 1984 at the time of the Los Angeles Olympics, with the intention of helping traffic flow'. Dodd-Thomas adds 'currently approximately 2200 managers at Pacific Bell telework – on an average of 1.5 days per week. We have four categories of teleworker: those who do it occasionally, those that do it all the time, those that do it part time and those that use a virtual office. 'Equipment and phone services are provided to the personnel dependent upon the percentage of time they telework. Usually they are provided with a telephone line and a lap-top that can be used in an office or at their home. Departments involved include: sales, internal auditing, programming, finance, marketing and operations.' She concludes, 'The benefits to Pacific Bell have included reduced costs in real estate (we plan on saving US$30 million in six years), increased productivity (sales people see on average two more customers each day) and improved customer service (due to the flexibility of teleworkers).

Going the extra mile for productivity

Flexibility and going that extra mile – or kilometre – for your company seems to be a feature of the teleworker. Organized, motivated and keen to prove their worth, they can – and do – deliver when tradition-bound office workers are strap-hanging their way home on crowded buses and trains.

Observes June Langhoff, a journalist and author of The Telecommuter's Advisor, 'Productivity increases because teleworkers experience less distraction at home, are able to work those flexible hours, suffer less stress and, as a result, of these desirable working conditions, stay highly motivated.' She continues, 'Because teleworkers will work with a cold or other minor ailment that might keep them away from the office, they usually work longer hours and more workdays than the average employee. Absenteeism often drops by half and long-term disability benefits are often reduced.'

Teleworkers get back to work faster than office-bound employees after sick leave, claim most surveys. Additionally, pregnant teleworkers are recorded as taking less time off before and after the birth.

Langhoff's observations are backed up by similar experiences in Finland – a highly teleworked society – where studies at computer company Nokia Data and state-owned Finnish Telecom showed that teleworkers do more in the course of a day than office-bound employees. Juhani Pekkola, a senior researcher at Finland's Ministry of Labour, reports 'personnel's working hours increase as they spontaneously prolong their workdays by accomplishing time-consuming tasks'. Pekkola has noted that at the beginning, 'the way of working will change in such a way that telework will consume more and more time at the cost of one's leisure and private life. Later on, overtime work will be diminished.' He confidently forecasts a future where 'the job contents will become much more interesting as teleworkers tend to bring home professionally and personally challenging tasks. Employees' preoccupation with interesting and challenging tasks will lead to performances unheard of. Teleworking seems to be a way of working to be reckoned with.'

In Washington DC, freezing conditions kick-in emergency laws stopping offices opening – obliging an entire city to telework.

June Langhoff cites another area where having teleworkers on the payroll can reap major advantages: strikes, bad weather and natural disasters. 'Telework provides an employer with another major advantage,' she points out, 'that is only often realized when an emergency occurs. Because teleworkers can work in a distributed fashion, often a company can keep going even if the offices are destroyed. For example, companies with telework programmes were able to get back in business within hours of the 1994 Northridge [Los Angeles] earthquake. And, after a fire shut down the Dallas Times Herald in Texas, journalists working from home were still able to get the newspaper out.'

Increased globalization of business can also be a boon to the teleworker. As Langhoff says, 'New York Life – an assurance company – has several computer programmers working from home, one of them in Nevada. And for anyone making real-time phone contact with clients around the world, who wants to get to work at four in the morning ?'

Telework – an encompassing concept

Three days after the 1994 Los Angeles earthquake, Pacific Bell were able to offer a complete telecommuting relief package. Used by more than 6000 individuals, it featured an advice hot-line, free installation on services to facilitate teleworking and a US$1 million equipment loan programme.

Telecom provider, AT&T, is another champion of the teleworker concept and its own experiences have been highly successful. In an introduction to its view on telework, AT&T clearly states the advantages for both employer and employee. 'Teleworking,' they say, 'is an encompassing concept. It redefines the traditional understanding of a workplace. It's all about flexible work arrangements that benefit and empower the employee. Teleworking might mean traveling an electronic highway, by bringing your work to you instead of getting into the car to travel to the office. 'Teleworking can be a regular agreement, where you work from home on specific days each week, or from a satellite office closer to home. The definition of teleworking may even expand to a permanent work-at-home arrangement for remotely deployed or disabled employees and any worker whose productivity is not determined by their presence at a specific business site. Implicit in teleworking's broadest definition is the concept of the virtual office – where technology combines portable/mobile computing and communications power to allow people to work virtually anywhere. Working in a virtual office environment means working from the customer's site, a home-based office, the hotel and even from trains and planes. Remember: teleworking means flexibility.

Use teleworking to solve business problems such as increasing overhead costs, demand for additional office and parking space, helping employees balance the demands of work and family and attracting and retaining the best talent for your business. These are just a few of the challenges facing companies around the world. It's clear the flexibility of teleworking can offer wide-ranging, powerful business solutions.'

Building up to telework

Telework isn't just working from a home base, or commuting a few days a week from a home base to a fixed place of work. Thousands of workers every day head out of their homes for a new location, where they may work supervised or unsupervised for a week and month or however long it takes to complete an assignment. Other days they may stay home and work on filing, record keeping, invoicing – that sort of thing.

One industry that operates like that but has little history of telework is the construction industry. But in Denmark, the Danish Master Builders' Organization have experimented with a network approach for small building firms. The results which are worth keeping in mind for anyone embarking on some type of telework system for employees not usually linked by PCs or modems show that there are definite differences between telework for absentee managers and company specialists and the stark reality of a building site.

These are the perceptions of the owners of a small Danish building contractor introduced to teleworking:

The downside

■ The real costs are expensive, even prohibitive to link all the people on all the sites.

■ It is also expensive to train people in a small company and maintain their knowledge.

■ There needs to be a substantial drop in prices to make it viable to groups like this.

■ The intent was that each building site would have a workstation. It didn't work like that: computers are personal – that is, they follow the person!

■ We had to overcome initial shyness, many builders do not spell all that well.

■ It helped us to realize that builders are not just responsible for good workmanship, today other skills are required as well.

Who teleworks and why?

The upside

- Sixty intelligent document formats have been developed in Lotus Notes, covering quality assurance, time sheets, agreement slips, weather conditions and so on.

- There was real enthusiasm, employees attended external courses, gave up leisure time to learn.

- Staff taking part in projects now have a feeling of belonging together. Now the rest of the staff want the training too!

- E-mail was used as an informal tool, almost as a telephone.

- Planning and management have become easier – and we were not quite so dependent on time and place.

- It has taken a lot of pressure off the main office.

- The building sites now take more direct responsibility.

Trivia note for construction workers!: a trackball mouse is not appropriate at a building site. Get a suitcase that holds the PC and a portable printer or put the installation in the cabin of your truck!

In fact it may well be that we have only begun to scratch the surface of telework options, but if we don't spend time trying, our competitors are more than likely to come up with innovations instead. In Japan an entrepreneur has opened a telework office that combines work with a resort setting to help employees recover from fatigue; in Sweden managers have experimented with an office train where they can work during their daily commute on half-pay. Elsewhere, many airlines have discovered that full-fare business passengers are not just aerial commuters but teleworkers and are busily installing business centres in lounges as well as phones and faxes on their aircraft. All across the French autoroute network, rest-stops have fax facilities.

Seemingly anyone who wants to – or can convince their boss it's a good idea – can telework, at least for part of their working life. However, we might be only limited by our imaginations, but the reality is that it is still the same old jobs that people suggest as those that are most suited. Pacific Bell's Guidelines and Consideration manual lists eighteen:

- Accounting
- Analysis
- Data entry
- Computer programming
- Project management
- Record keeping

- Course development
- Planning and budgeting
- Systems engineering
- Administrative work/advertising
- Auditing report

- Data processing
- Legal work
- Research
- Market analysis
- Sales
- Telemarketing
- Word processing

The Market Research Institute in a telework survey in late 1995 came up with a top eight executive positions suitable for telework:

- Customer service representative
- Human resource professional
- Information specialist
- General manager

- Market research analyst
- Programmer
- Sales representative
- Systems analyst

Telework improves flexibility

What all these lists seem to fail to take into account is that telework isn't just one thing, one set of work that you can do at home, or another away-from-the-office location. It might be an agreed amount of time in days away from your usual desk or it might be as the need arises. But every single one of us in the new working world, where we are being urged to think flexible, needs to consider this as an option – however infrequent.

In fact, few people can read and create amid a noisy office atmosphere. And that – apart from sales people – is what teleworkers seem to use most of their homework time for. A study by the Washington State Energy Office asked teleworkers what they most often did on their days working at home:

Read	68%	Record keeping	26%
Write	67%	Design	15%
Word process	62%	Computer program	14%
Analysis	47%	Administration	13%
Phone	38%	Teach or train	3%
Problem solve	36%	Meetings	2%

This shows that the average office worker – not the sales or service professional – is using one or two days per week as 'quiet time' to catch up with things they need to know, write reports and learn new skills and update themselves on software and other professional needs.

in brief.

'The nature of work – and the workplace – has changed dramatically over the last two decades. These changes, evolutionary from a technological standpoint and revolutionary in creating a new realm of management issues, have resulted in both the opportunity and the need for flexible work arrangements.'
– **Hal Burlingame, senior vice president, human resources, AT&T**

A glimpse of teleworker heaven?

Any organization or individual signing up for a telework experiment needs to know where an ultimate extension of ten or twelve employees working from home two or three days a week can get you. Canby, a small community about 25 miles outside Portland, Oregon is held up as possibly the most teleworked place in the world (Appendix 6 at the end of the book also contains a proposed telecommunity.)

The community (with a population that hovers around the 10 000 mark) has set itself the task of becoming the first total telecommunity in which everyone uses technology to work, educate and govern. Charles Grantham, president of the Institute for the Study of Distributed Work, who is helping the so-called *Canbyites* develop the concept, says that soon a typical work-week could look something like this:

- Two days a week a *Canbyite* might work at home, using a computer, modem and fax machine to work with a company located outside the community.
- For one or two other days the worker might go over to a local school, where a teleworker centre has been installed. This telework centre will be equipped with everything from cubicles outfitted with computers, modems, faxes and printers to complete video-conferencing facilities. Several companies would lease individual space for use by different employees on different days. The teleworker might come in for a video-conference with co-workers or clients in Portland, New York, Japan or Sweden, meet with some colleagues or even participate in a class for an hour or two.
- Another day each week might involve physical commuting into Portland for a staff meeting or other on-site work.

Grantham enthuses that 'this project involves far more than just new ways to work. The community is actively working on plans for technologically interactive government and education as well as identifying ways to attract the kinds of people who would find the envisioned lifestyle/workstyle appealing.'

However, out in the real world teleworkers are getting on with their working lives, and each of them is different: different work expectations, different responsibilities, different job content. Based on research with Irish teleworkers, here's how jobs can differ:

Part-time, home-based teleworker

- Female typist working for a consultancy firm on a part-time basis, so that she can care for a pre-school child at home. **Important!** Most teleworker experts stress that telework should not be seen by individuals or employees as a substitute for day-care for children or other arrangements.
- Mostly used to cover work peaks at the firm
- Visits office twice a week to pick up work (dictation tapes or manuscripts) and deliver typed work on floppy disks

- Informal contract, payment is made per number of hours worked
- Contract between teleworker and managing director of company
- Workload and deadlines are negotiated on an individual job basis between company and worker
- PC is owned by teleworker who looks after her own health and safety, i.e. adequacy of office equipment, lighting, heating
- The company does not reimburse any other expenses.

Telecottages

- Local centres equipped with latest information technology (e.g. computers, fax machines and photocopying equipment) which provides a telecommunications facility for small businesses, self-employed and computer students
- Publicly funded
- Telecottages aim to develop awareness of IT through training on systems
- Keep records for small companies on computer at telecottage which can only be accessed by telecottage staff
- Some telecottages provide additional services like desktop publishing and colour photocopying for small businesses.

Centre-based telemarketing and telesales

- European facility of a US computer manufacturer, providing telemarketing, telesales and technical support for customers in Ireland and other European countries
- Teleworkers work from a centre and have a standard contract similar to other employees
- Workers are paid on a monthly basis and receive a commission on sales
- Health and safety conditions are the same as for other employees.

So where are the downsides?

So are there any downsides to teleworking? Most companies seem to have had or at least report nothing but good experiences from their attempts to introduce a more open, flexible style of work – at the very least no one has offered evidence of any complete disasters.

Of course, there will always be one or two employees who betray the trust shown in them, just as there will be the odd unscrupulous employer who tries to use telework as a way to divest obligations and job protection. A BT report, The Economics of Teleworking, says that 'most organizations could introduce teleworking to some degree. Exceptions to the rule spring to mind – sometimes only to be confounded by innovative companies.' BT's report points out that 'it is obvious retailers must staff their shops and meet the public face-to-face. Yet some major retailers are exploring teleworking and catalogues replace shops with mail-order. It is unlikely that production lines could be redesigned to enable cars to be made at home. But a car designed for Third World nations purports to do just that.' They add, 'Bar staff clearly could not telework, nor could North Sea divers. A footballer could not telework, nor could a tour guide.'

OK, perhaps the footballer couldn't, but today's technology allows for a lot. North Sea divers, knowing what to look for, could remotely explore the sea bed while sitting in an office, tour guides could be on-line to Paris and Rome from a leafy lane in London. As we said, it's only the imagination that restricts what the telework phenomenon can do.

That's the management challenge, to be aware of the technological implications, see how they apply to the present business and assess what the cost/benefit equation would be if you began a process of telework for those it would benefit most. In a world where productivity is crucial and managing overhead just as important, anything that can impact the bottom line is a precious commodity indeed. Teleworking, properly structured and managed is just that.

Executive Summary

- Telework isn't just a solo activity it can be a whole new system-built unit.

- Telework will only work in countries that have the right infrastructure, technology and skilled personnel.

- Teleworking, mobile employees are redefining what we call the office.

- Telework is saving money and increasing sales – that's what it's all about.

- Telework is available to a lot more people than we think. We are limited only by our imaginations.

- Telework is still dominated by the jobs that need peace and quiet, thinking and writing.

4

The do's and don'ts of teleworking

Despite the fact that teleworking has been recognized as a potentially useful flexible work tool by almost everyone, in many companies it is still, surprisingly, stuck in the starting blocks or confined to the slow lane. In reality, few corporations have really got teleworking up and running at full speed on the fast track. The reasons for this are as myriad as the possible applications for telework, but in most cases they come down to an inability for individual managers or an entire senior management group to think outside the present organizational system.

Managers might be being urged and encouraged to look outside the organizational boxes they have been confined to for so long under command and control management styles and search for better ways to achieve their goals. But many are reluctant to give it a go, especially with an experiment like teleworking where one of the main objectives is to empower workers. Indeed, many hard-pressed, scared executives are unwilling to lose any sort of control over the people they supervise. In departments and strategic business units like these, teleworking is just not an option.

Six do's and two don'ts

There is a lot more advice of what *to do* and what *not to do* in this chapter, but here are eight pieces of advice offered by the Institute of Management's Flexible Working Practices and Homeworking Guide:

■ *Do* convince line managers of the business benefits of teleworking *before* it is introduced.

■ *Do* find ways of motivating and providing social contact for teleworkers.

■ *Do* ensure that line managers are in daily contact with teleworking staff.

■ *Do* provide adequate training in handling new equipment and ensure back-up services.

■ *Do* make teleworking available at all levels and within all suitable functions.

■ *Do* review the staff and the jobs open to teleworking on a regular basis.

■ *Don't* consider teleworking as an alternative to child care.

■ *Don't* make assumptions about which staff will want to become teleworkers.

Further up the command chain, senior managers are also believed to be reluctant in many cases to try out teleworking and others forms of flexible employment, also fearing that once let loose, employees will escape from their control. Although hundreds of test cases indicate the exact opposite, showing that responsible, empowered employees actually blossom and grow when allowed to, there are still many companies where old-fashioned work practices rule.

Possibly one of the biggest concerns of dyed-in-the-wool managers, who haven't heard there's a work revolution afoot, is the loss of control issue. The 'if I can't see them, I

Memorandum to all managers! When your staff are in the office can you actually see them working all the time? No, of course not! So what's the difference between them working at home or in the office? How many times a day do you pick up the phone and say, 'can you come and *see* me?' when you could just as easily talk on the phone.

won't know if they are working or not' syndrome is remarkably alive and well, and doing an excellent job in getting us nowhere **fast**. What needs to happen is for senior managers or external consultants and trainers to explain to worried managers and supervisors that they are not giving up power and control, they just have to look at it, and measure it in another way. If they can be made to see that it will enhance their department's or team's results they can usually be talked round.

One of the major problems is that teleworking gets off to a bad start, because it all began as a way of helping out one or two individuals – definitely not the way to get started! Unorganized, informal and often done in secret – all hell usually breaks out when things get out into the open.

Imagine, if you will, this scenario. A valued worker persuades her supervisor to let her stay home and work several times a week – it allows her to keep a better eye on her elderly parents, or some such Good Samaritan reason. The supervisor, knowing he can trust the person, agrees. All goes well for some months, until co-workers realize that their colleague is making a permanent situation out of this new work practice. Possibly tired of taking her calls when she is not around, they too demand the right to work from home if they want.

The result is a brief period of chaos, management intervention and the torpedoing of the idea. No one has the temerity to raise the idea again. Experiences like this are legion. One false move condemns a great idea before it has had any chance to even make it to the formal level – even as an experiment.

Similar cases have been recorded with sales staff setting off directly from home every morning for far-away sales calls instead of going into the office first; and of service and customer care employees doing the same thing. The lesson to be learned is not that teleworking – or distance working – is bad, just make sure that your supervisor or whoever is in charge of your workgroup has explained what's happening to a superior. Formalizing a work relationship makes all the difference.

in brief

'Telecommuting is the technosocial megatrend that never happened. . . the irony is that just as the technology has become good enough and cheap enough to allow enormous numbers of people to work from home there is more frustration than ever among both employees and managers'
— **David Bjerklie, *Technology Review,***

eleworking cannot be een as a standalone ctivity. It is part of the rganization and has to e managed as an itegrated piece of the usiness.

But, at the end of the day, if senior management haven't approved it and preferably thought it up for themselves (or at least believe they invented it!) teleworking, like other organizational experiments, is probably doomed to failure. Writing in Management Consultancy magazine, David Skyrme, a UK-based management systems consultant with a broad experience in teleworking systems, offered some key pointers on managerial involvement as a important factor in the success or failure of telework and other flexible work trials. Here's a modified version of his views:

■ Do make sure that you understand the prevailing business environment, especially the cost-drivers and the opportunities afforded by location-independent work.

■ Do make certain that telework is seen as part of an overall flexible working and human resources response to those cost-drivers.

Teleworking

- ■ Do make sure that the organization understands that telework is not about people working full-time from home or telecentres. It is about working in the most appropriate environments for the tasks in hand.

- ■ Do make sure that a successful telework programme needs a business champion. Having a senior director participating as a teleworker gives added bite and credibility.

- ■ Do make it clear that employees must have involvement in decision making from the outset. Teleworking should not be imposed on individuals without their consent – use incentives, not threats.

- ■ Do encourage creative and unorthodox ways of thinking about better ways of working.

- ■ Do push for experimentation. The most successful telework schemes all started with a number of small, pilot projects.

- ■ Do bring in external advisers and facilitators to provide an objective and independent perspective.

- ■ Do regularly review expectations, achievements, problems and lessons learned.

- ■ Do remember to continually improve and adjust telework systems and procedures to meet changing needs in the marketplace.

Using this as a kick-off checklist for any flexible work initiative will involve management at a proper level and also make it clear to the whole organization that telework experiments are to be taken seriously throughout the business. Top management enthusiasm and continued interest are still the best discouragers of dissent no matter what corporate culture we might live in.

AT&T, mindful of the problems of supervising teleworking, have come up with their version of Do's and Don'ts that is very useful for anyone who has the responsibility for controlling those workers who may be out of sight, but shouldn't be out of mind.

Do's and don'ts for the successful supervisor

- Do guide your entire workgroup through a series of 'what if' scenarios. Come up with workable solutions as a team.

- Do trust your teleworkers.

- Do require teleworkers to participate in surveys and evaluations – and participate yourself.

- Do use teleworking as an opportunity to strengthen your own management skills.

- Do manage by measuring results – schedule regular status reports.

- Do telework yourself, when you have the opportunity. It will help increase your personal effectiveness and improve your understanding of the ups and downs of telework.

- Do look at things from your teleworker's point of view. Understand time-frames involved in completing tasks and the resources required to complete them.

- Do include your teleworkers in goal-setting.

- Do delegate assignments fairly among teleworkers and non-teleworkers.

- Do include the teleworkers in day-to-day activities; keep on the look-out for clues that a teleworker is feeling isolated, left out or has cabin fever.

- Do expect that things might not go smoothly all the time.

- Do communicate on a regular basis; let the teleworker know you're there for them.

- Do be willing and prepared to increase the frequency of teleworking, if it is working well for the employee.

Teleworking

■ Do be prepared to let the employee terminate the programme – or terminate it yourself – if it is clearly not working out.

■ Do keep an open mind about teleworking – if one arrangement doesn't work, it doesn't mean the next one won't.

■ Do communicate!

■ Don't conduct curfew checks.

■ Don't call your teleworkers every hour to check on progress.

■ Don't ignore your teleworker either.

■ Don't ask for constant status reports.

Trust issues also impact those that are not teleworking. They need to trust that teleworkers will meet their commitments and be as accessible as they are in the office or won't offload tasks onto them.

■ Don't expect unrealistic deadlines for projects.

■ Don't neglect problems.

■ Don't set unattainable goals.

■ Don't manage by close supervision.

■ Don't expect perfection, there will be adjustments.

■ Don't allow one unsuccessful attempt to give teleworking a bad name.

■ Don't expect everyone to be a successful teleworker

Do's and don'ts for the successful employee

At the personal level, just what should the employer expect of the individual? Tempting as it may be to check up on what they are doing, we have to remember that there is nothing wrong with them walking the dog at ten in the morning, or playing golf at three in the afternoon, if they are working at other times and getting their work done. Remember, telework is built on trust and on what gets done by a specific deadline, not when the person is working. All the same, companies might want to consider – as suggested earlier – that staff are available at certain specified times during the day to answer queries and be able to link up to fellow teleworkers. Obviously customer-support staff – whose job is the phone or data link – have to be on call for specific time periods.

Based on input from a broad base of European and US organizations who have active telework programmes, here is a do's and dont's checklist for the individual worker – especially those staying home-alone:

Little is known about the ype of teleworkers hey employ, but one company has a home-worker's handbook that warns against:

- Snacking too much
- Oversleeping
- Making long personal phones calls
- Watching TV
- Drinking alcoholic beverages
- Visiting the neighbours
- Procrastinating

■ Do have a specific, dedicated, comfortable workplace or workstation at home, that is private and as secluded as possible from the day-to-day domestic hustle and bustle of the rest of the family. Ideally it should have a door that can be closed and locked.

■ Do develop a beginning of the work-day ritual and stay with it. It could be taking the dog for a ten-minute walk, watering the plants, reading the newspaper for ten minutes, downloading your e-mail and responding to it.

■ Do the same thing at the end of the working day – a habit you form – and always try to end at a logical break point when a task is complete.

■ Do make sure you stick to the same schedule on both telework and office commute days.

■ Do make sure – like long car trips – you take a stretch and rest break during the day. Stop and call a friend, agree a lunch or dinner date, book those theatre or concert tickets.

■ Do keep your workplace tidy and don't drag your papers through the house. Oil-spills are ugly at sea, paper-spills do the same for a house.

■ Do plan the teleworking days at home well ahead, so you know what you'll be doing. Have a file, a dedicated brief-case, even a plastic bag, to drop in any papers or other material you'll need.

■ Do determine just how many interruptions you can take. If you don't want any, set that as a standard and keep to it. Once family, friends and neighbours see you sticking to it they'll respect it.

■ Do make sure that your family are fully supportive of your plan and that they understand – really understand – what is involved.

■ Do realize that you will sacrifice: access to support services, visibility from senior management and the physical contact of your colleagues.

■ Do be prepared to have reduced living space at home.

■ Do be prepared to be responsible for 'home' security of files, equipment, products and samples.

■ Do call the office and talk to your supervisor and your co-workers to let them know you're there and how you are progressing, but don't overdo it to impress them how busy or efficient you are. Don't get paranoid that you are on your own and not back at the office.

■ Do participate in office meetings, either physically or by conference or video call as often as possible. Be seen to be an interested, active member of the team. Also do make sure you keep in touch with other teleworking co-workers – ask their advice and listen to their experiences.

■ Do stick to all deadlines. It's important to show that you can meet – and exceed – goals that have been set for you, especially in the first months.

Two teleworkers at home isn't a great recipe for success. Teleworking wives report having problems convincing husbands that also telework that they are not available to cook or go shopping.

Don't worry too much about company equipment being secure. That is often safer in a teleworker's home than in the traditional office where items are easily stolen and visitors can easily read confidential documents on desks.

80

The do's and dont's of teleworking

- Do let your manager know if telework really isn't for you. . .but

- Do give teleworking a chance. It's a big step for many, and it takes time to appreciate its pros and cons.

Now a few don'ts for employees to consider:

- Don't sit in bed or laze on the sofa to do your work – and get dressed too! This may sound silly, but you need a proper workplace and need to be aware and alert and enthusiastic. All the same, don't be afraid to dress casually and comfortably either.

- Don't make a habit of sleeping late on telework days.

- Don't put off doing things. It can be easier to develop bad work habits when you are teleworking. Set yourself goals you have to achieve by a specific time, before a coffee break, before lunch, before quitting for the day.

- Don't let the TV or radio, or your latest CD distract you. Background music can be soothing for some, rock 'n' roll doesn't quite work out. Oh, and don't work with your Walkman headphones stuck in your ears either!

espite the increasing number of teleworkers here is still a stigma ot unlike – until the ecessions of the late 980s – there used to e with being unemployed. Stories bound of wives trying, ut failing, to ccommodate their usband's new home-ased work-pattern. ccusations of 'when re you going to go out nd get a proper job?' re more common than any realize.

- Don't work at home if you are not getting along with your spouse or other family members. Rows and distractions are a sure way to make sure your productivity takes a nose dive. Pull your papers together and head for the office. Also, don't work at home if you have a baby, toddler or elderly relative who needs constant care and attention. Telework is not a substitute for alternative home-based care.

- Don't take work that requires group decisions or input from other team members home on telework days – unless you can solve issues on-line.

- Don't be put off discussing any telework-related problems you may have with your manager.

- Don't continue in the teleworking programme if you've given it a chance and it's not working for you. Remember, teleworking doesn't work for everybody.

Make sure the employee is suited to telework

Finally, here's a list that both employer and employee need to consider before embarking on telework. It's crucial to remember that not everyone is suited:

Do make sure the potential teleworker:
- Is self-motivated
- Exhibits a positive, eager attitude toward telework
- Is well organized
- Already has a high level of productivity
- Requires a minimum of supervision
- Gets on well with their family members
- Prefers the home environment
- Is moderately people/social oriented
- Has a high level of skill and knowledge of the work
- Exhibits strong time-management skills

Remember, not everyone wants to be a teleworker. Lots of people like sitting for two hours morning and evening in the warm cocoon of their car, listening to the radio, talking books, foreign-language tapes or just lost in their own private world.

While it might seem that there are an awful lot of things you, as an employer or employee, need to do; a lot of points that you need to remember before you can become an effective teleworker, don't let that put you or your employees off the idea. The important thing is to create your own system out of those do's and don'ts. Everyone's circumstances – both professional and personal – are different, and they need to apply sensible rules that work for them. One size, does not fit everyone.

If we stop to consider it, all of us have to accept, come to terms with and work within the rules, the policies, the systems and the procedures of traditional office life. Telework frees people up from much of that. So, although we need basic rules and guidelines to govern telework, employees are – in reality – much freer to set their own standards, to work the way they want than they ever could be in the nine-to-five communal office environment. Even in telecentres, working rules tend to be more relaxed.

All the same, any serious organization is going to demand and get guarantees that work will be done on time and to a certain standard, as well as insisting that working conditions are up to scratch. Remember that many teleworking

employees are on the payroll and the company is liable –
at least to some extent in most countries – for ensuring that
the place of work is adequate for the tasks they are being
asked to do. And it is important for both employer and
employee to set out standards to ensure this. The last thing
any promising telework project needs is a problem with
either health and safety inspectors or corporate legal staff.

Take a professional approach

separate their private
from their professional
life, teleworkers have
one as far as dressing
up in a suit and tie,
icking up their
briefcase, leaving the
ouse, walking round the
lock, re-entering the
ouse and going up to
he office. At the end of
he day they do the same
hing in reverse and,
rriving 'home;' change
to casual clothes.

What is probably most important with telework, as with most
other forms of flexible working, is that a professional
approach is taken to the concept and the execution by both
employer and employee. Agreeing on the standards, setting
down the rules, knowing what each side expects of the
other may take time, but it will pay off in the longer term.
And it pays to get the initial guidelines right from the beginning, for if a telework experiment is a success and it is
decided to continue and expand the system to other
employees it is difficult to then stop and set up new rules
and regulations. So do get it right from the outset. Don't wait
until it's too late.

Selling the telework concept to the organization

Another way of determining that your telework programme
is going to get the full attention it deserves is to follow advice
offered by Pacific Bell. Concerned that their managers and
supervisors get as involved as possible with the whole
telework issue from the outset they recommend some things
that all of us should take into account when we plan and
champion our telework project:

■ Do sell the programme constantly. Clear understanding
and constant promotion of the benefits of teleworking are

essential. By managing the project you will acquire a global perspective.

- Do spread the word about teleworking. Be creative and use every available means of communication.

- Do pursue and promote a champion of teleworking. If there is a department currently using teleworking, pursue that group and persuade them to join the effort in formalizing teleworking for the whole organization.

- Do become the subject-matter expert. Get involved with telework professional associations and keep up to date with news and research on new applications.

- Do provide vision. Teleworking is an educational process and resistance may exist because of a lack of understanding. Be aware of the changing needs of your working environment and how telework can help meet those needs. Be creative in developing and applying new telework applications for your organization.

Keeping teleworkers happy is a key requirement. One organization seeks to keep them amused as well and has created fun phrases for serious issues. For example, their on-line help desk for distant workers is called 'Mouse-to-Mouse Resuscitation!'

- Do encourage part-time telework. The most successful prototype programmes have had teleworkers at home one or two days per week. Very few individuals can successfully stay at home five days a week, for many, complete isolation from the office environment has inherent drawbacks that should be avoided.

- Do establish deadlines. It is imperative to have a plan, but be flexible enough to allow for dates to be changed. Encouraging everyone to participate will afford ownership and accountability to your test programme.

- Do practise what you preach. You need to work at least one day a week at home in order to obtain first-hand experience about teleworking. Assign time on your own agenda for regular teleworking.

84

5

The management issues of telework for organizations and individuals

A survey by UK tele-communications giant BT on why companies reject telework concluded 'possibly the most compelling reason is the amount of capital tied up in offices, company cars, existing communications and employment practices. But in the rapidly evolving world economy of the 20th century, organizations, like the products and services they offer, must adapt or they will rapidly become extinct.'

Most often, management enjoy blaming employees for the inability to get things done. 'They can't or won't change,' is the frequent cry of frustrated managers, desperate to find new directions for their companies. But when it comes to telework it is often the reverse. Managers and supervisors are the people who can't or won't change, usually citing lack of control and concerns about work productivity as their reasons for eyeing telework with considerable suspicion. Others, concerned that they have too much capital tied up in factories and office buildings, are reluctant to change the status quo. But as everyone knows, hesitation in the face of the economic and social changes we are going through can be disastrous. Telework – and variations of it – may not be the only solution, but it is a very distinct part of the work revolution. And with technology and cost breakthroughs making it ever more viable, organizations can ignore these sweeping developments at their peril.

There is a further consideration, not often raised in the telework debate. Too many managers – particularly those at senior level – are still carrying out their daily tasks in blissful ignorance of the technology revolution around them. Like the First World War, with generals planning skirmishes, attacks and complete campaigns based on cavalry horses not tanks, they are unaware of the power that is flowing through the desktops of their employees.

Don't overestimate a manager's knowledge of telework

Result? Many managers are unable to join in the telework debate, because they don't know what it can do for them, because they haven't kept up with the technology. This is one area where enthusiasts and promoters of telework tend to come unstuck. They overestimate the level of understanding of a large group of managers – the 45- to 60-year-olds – who are often the key decision makers when it comes to human resource allocation and budgetary considerations.

Managing telework centres

Telework centres are a growing part of how many organizations are making a successful transition to a more flexible work pattern for their employees. While there are many different types of telework centre, they usually have two things in common: a desire to bring work closer to people and reduce long-commutes into city centres and other high-density traffic locations and a belief that employees will work better in a telework centre – with the social interaction of other people – than on their own at home.

Typically, telework centres break up into four types:
- Those wholly owned by a single business for distributing work to a local community area
- Those owned by a group of companies, who see the need of a jointly owned telework centre to save and share office and technology costs

- Those created by a local government authority to attract business to an often rural location
- Those owned by an entrepreneur, who leases out space and facilities by the day, week, month or year to local companies and organizations and may also provide computing services.

However, companies that have experienced telecentre working practices have learned that there are some vital points to take into consideration when either setting up or taking space in a facility. Based on the experiences of several organizations, as well as a report from the Washington State Telework Centre, here are a few points that make sense to follow.

- Employers should consider reducing the number of workstations at the main office. This will require teleworkers to share their workstation and perhaps use a different workstation on different days. Reducing the amount of workstations in the main office allows organizations to provide employee workstations at the telecentre without an increase in hardware and software costs. For an organization that does this while also implementing a home telework programme, the potential for cost savings on central office space and associated services can be considerable.
- The actual location of a telework centre is critical for the viability of the operation. The centre – by its location – should significantly reduce the commute of employees working from the centre (or provide a workplace for new employees, who would not normally be available to you), so should be close to, or in, major residential areas or have a significant amount of traffic passing by to syphon-off employees and reduce their commutes. The centre should also be served by adequate public transport and be close to shops, banks and restaurants.
- The design and services on offer at the telecentre will significantly determine the ability of the location to attract employers and their employees. While it is difficult in the initial period to anticipate the needs and usage of employers and employees, every effort should be made to do so. It should be taken into account that users may require private office space, meeting rooms, secure storage areas and secure communications systems. Thought should also be given to limiting access to non-centre users.

■ Employers may wish to reserve space or workstations annually, while others may want to use them only on a daily basis. Accommodating different employers and employees will greatly increase the success of the telecentre.

■ Individual workstations need to be of a flexible design to accommodate different teleworkers. Care should be taken to ensure that teleworkers have user-friendly link-ups to their networks. A basic workstation should be equipped with a computer (although it should be taken into account that many teleworkers will bring their own lap-top), access to a printer, work-surface areas, filing cabinets and storage capacity. Links to e-mail services should be provided as well as a telephone with voice-mail facilities.

■ A conference room complete with audio-visual and tele/video conference facilities should be considered when planning a telecentre. This can be particularly useful for organizations who want to ensure that all their employees stay informed of major announcements.

■ The centre – depending on the size of the facility – may also require a lunch room, cooking facilities, hot beverage and cold drink facilities and a refrigerator and microwave so employees can prepare their own meals.

■ Support staff at a telecentre should include a technical specialist (or one on 24-hour call who is located within easy reach). A receptionist or secretarial/administrative support may also be included depending on the nature of the work being carried out. Support personnel can significantly increase costs. Employers should consider alternative solutions like transmitting materials to central office for processing.

■ Training employees to use a telecentre is vital, especially in all aspects of the use of the equipment, security of office systems and the centre itself.

■ Management should consider setting minimum use levels on any telecentre to track whether it is a useful and profitable addition to their operations. Employees – who may spend part of their time on the road or working from home or other locations – should be told of the usage guidelines.

Remember whatever you do, the costs of establishing a new facility can be considerably higher – particularly in the initial stages – than using existing facilities or allowing employees to telecommute from home. Also, if you are a private entrepreneur creating a telecentre, or a company that wants to share costs with another organization, don't forget that you may have to spend considerable time marketing the virtues of your operation. Jobs and needs change rapidly and to make a telecentre a success plans have to be created that will assume a high turnover of users.

Now here are another few tips for assessing the practicality and usage of a telecentre. These can apply to organization or individuals:

- ■ Visit the intended centre site and check out if it has:
  - Adequate transportation access
  - Parking and location convenience
  - Access to shops and stores that suit the centre's users
- ■ Visit the centre and check:
  - If it is adequately equipped
  - That the workstations are comfortable
  - That the physical environment meets your needs (lighting, noise level, ventilation, privacy)
  - What extras you will need to provide
- ■ Ask about current and future pricing and compare it with other telecentres if possible. What is their current occupancy level and why? Can you get increased space if you require it later?
- ■ How do the costs fit in with your budget? Can you make it cost-effective?
- ■ Finally, examine all the aspects of telecommunication capability and how it will, or will not, meet the needs of your business

Nicholas Negroponte, founder of the MIT Media Labs, and author of the hugely successful book, Being Digital, calls this generation 'the digitally homeless'. He points out that at present, until the next generation – which will be digitally literate – takes over, the people who run our governments, make our laws and run our institutions and companies belong to this digitally homeless generation. They have grown up and made their entire careers without having to worry about the computer.

Almost like the typewriter, computers are viewed by many senior managers as things for secretaries and clerks to play with and if you want to promote teleworking as a concept you had better believe it. Think about it. Few managers are on the end of their personal e-mail number like Bill Gates at Microsoft. In fact few senior managers have embraced the possibilities of the digital revolution in any depth on an individual basis. So before you try to sell your telework idea, make sure that top management understand exactly what you are talking about.

Jack Nilles, one of the leading spokespeople for the telework revolution, refers to the current status of many corporations as the 'edifice complex'. Suggesting that many corporations have to have an impressive office building in order to show off their wealth and prestige, he charges that without the 'edifice complex' many more people would work from home.

Support for this argument of convincing those at the top comes from Jack Nilles, known as the father of telecommuting. He is on record as saying 'It's like the old real estate adage location, location, location: the primary barriers to teleworking are management, management, management. The reason that managers are loath to adopt teleworking is simple, it's scary to be in the position of managing people you can't see, especially if you manage by walking around. So the first step in starting teleworking in an organization is to convince managers that teleworking is in their best interests as well as those of the teleworkers.' Nilles adds, 'This isn't something you decide to do one day and start doing the next. Successful teleworking requires some careful planning, some attention to technology, to liability and other legal issues, selection of teleworkers and telemanagers (not everyone can do it) and training. Teleworking involves cultural change in most organizations – that takes time and persistence. Typically it can take two years to get a teleworking programme started in a large organization and another year or three to go from demonstration stage to a roll-out to the rest of the company.'

in brief
'...many managers worry that employees may miss the social interaction of the traditional office environment ... the solution may be to create a virtual water-cooler, using today's available equipment and technology.'
– Ken Radziwanowski, AT&T School of Business

Another of telecommute/telework's icons, Gil Gordon, who has championed rethinking the workplace for decades, is even harder on reluctant managers. 'One reason why so many managers find it hard to accept teleworking is because they never learned to manage correctly and they had decades of poor role models who reinforced activity-based supervision instead of results-based management.'

Keep it legal

Employers planning a telework programme need to keep in mind that in most countries their at-home staff will be covered by specific work regulations. Laws are in force stipulating minimum requirements for a healthy and safe home-work area. In most countries, health and safety officials will make a point of visiting teleworkers' homes to check on compliance. Basic requirements in most countries are:

- **VDU display screen should swivel and tilt easily**

- **Keyboard should be adjustable and sufficient space should be provided to support the hands and arms of the user**

- **Desk should be sufficiently large for the tasks required with sufficient space for legs and knees**

- **Chair should be adjustable in height, including the back rest, and a foot rest should be made available if required**

- **Environmental factors that can be assessed include effects from reflection, glare, heat, cold noise and humidity**

Also keep in mind that in many countries employers do not have the right to inspect a teleworker's 'office' space unless it is pre-agreed in the work contract although they may be liable for work and equipment safety and maintenance.

The recipe for the ideal manager in the new teleworker world

Gil Gordon – whose newsletter Telecommuting Review, is a 'must read' for telework professionals everywhere – suggests the ingredients of an alternative manager for the new work realities of the late 1990s. 'If I were going to dictate a recipe for the ideal manager, I'd add in one part purchasing manager, one-part field sales manager, one part general contractor and one part communications expert.' He adds, 'Let me explain those ingredients:

- The competent purchasing manager knows how to source, evaluate and negotiate with outside vendors, and how to create performance-based contracts for the goods or services to be provided.
- The competent field sales manager knows how to manage and motivate a dispersed team, how to understand the link between activity levels and the results that activity should produce, and how to influence a group of independent contributors to share expertise with each other, while allowing them to feel entrepreneurial.
- The competent general contractor knows how to break down a big task into discrete smaller tasks, how to manage a series of sequential and/or simultaneous events into an overall project plan and time line, and how to minimize conflicts among subcontractors whose own interests can and often do conflict with each others' and with those of the client.
- The competent communications expert is a master at choosing and using the right mix of personal, written and on-line communications tools to get the message across; knows how to set expectations and give feedback about progress against them, and how to persuade without patronizing and confront without bludgeoning.'

Management Technology Associates (MTA) point out that it is important for managers to get a 'realistic perspective of telework. Managers with direct experience emphasize the benefits to be gained and regard any issues as "problems to be solved,". Managers without experience tend to be strongly aware of what they regard as issues and drawbacks and only vaguely aware of the benefits. They see telework through the media image of a "country cottage lifestyle", and are largely unaware of the significant benefits to employers.'

What MTA advocate to managers who need to get acquainted is that 'the next time you have a concentrative task to finish, try staying at home for a day or half a day – all telework means at its simplest is "working at home when appropriate". Ask yourself what proportion of your work and your staff's work really is done best in a busy office and after commuting.'

All the same – as we have already referred to in previous chapters – it is not always just managers who are barriers to telework taking off. Society hasn't totally come to grips with telework as an option for the successful employee either. The man or woman who takes the car, train or bus every day is still seen as 'going to work'. The person who stays at home creates a totally different image which society as a whole is still coming to terms with – they need to try **very hard**.

Norwegian commentator and researcher on teleworking, John Bakke, is in no doubt that there is still a problem, 'regarding the societal acceptance of telework as a legitimate way of working, so there is a need to develop attractive ways of organizing telework'. Bakke is lucky; he lives in Scandinavia, which has not only embraced telework wholeheartedly (largely because it has an excellent technology infrastructure and a lot of well-educated rural dwellers) but looks set to be one of the world-wide winners: at least in the short and medium term. The reason is that the Scandinavian character and their culture were made for telework. Living in a very free, but well-regulated society, relatively crime-free, where laws are – in the most part – respected, Scandinavians are hard working, organized and highly numerate and literate. They also have a huge respect for the work/leisure/home equation. Telework comes almost naturally to them. It is a society where people can be and are treated as adults. Bakke highlights these traits, 'It is commonly acknowledged that some of the characteristic traits of working life include:

on't let phone nswering become a ustomer turn-off. nswering teleworker's hones while they are ot in the office-location hould not start with, 'Miss Smith is at home oday .....', try' Miss mith is unavailable at his time ....' instead.

Teleworking

- A fairly egalitarian atmosphere at work

- A large degree of discretion for the employees

- Participation in technology development and organizational development'

'All the traits mentioned,' Bakke suggests, 'seem suitable for the establishment of teleworking schemes. The first two points refer to trust and autonomy – properties that seem especially relevant for the running of teleworking schemes, since the teleworker has to some extent be his or her own manager. The latter point is important for the establishment or implementation of teleworking schemes.'

Moving managers from leaders to coordinators

Unhappy teleworkers are those that have least contact with their company. Managers must realize that ongoing two-way contact is important in keeping teleworkers interested and motivated.

What they have discovered about managing in the telework area is particularly useful for would-be adopters of this form of work-style. According to Bakke, 'the middle manager may have to take on tasks as a contact person for the teleworker, and provide administrative support beyond what we are used to at today's level. He or she must ensure that the coordination of work between teleworkers and office-based workers is taken care of, also keeping an eye on team relations and making sure that relationships to colleagues are maintained.' Bakke's view on all this is that the manager or supervisor's role will begin to change 'from being a leader to becoming more of a coordinator or facilitator, for instance in team-based organizations, where the role of the manager is more to influence team behaviour.' Would-be telework promoters may find that a visit to Scandinavia to see how it does it is not at all a bad idea.

In the USA, Pacific Bell's experiences coincide with Bakke's observations. They have found that 'just as critical to the success of a teleworking arrangement is the role of the managing supervisor. As with a teleworker, there are prevalent traits which help to make telework work. They are:

■ An open, positive attitude towards teleworking

■ A mutual trust and respect in ongoing relations with the teleworker

■ Above-average organizational and planning skills

■ The ability to establish clear objectives and measurement and to evaluate results

■ The provision of regular feedback

■ Facilitates an open channel for communication

■ An innovative and flexible approach to managing subordinates.'

Natalie Fay of the Bay Area Telecommuting Assistance Project in California makes some further suggestions when it comes to supervisors measuring job performance. 'A successful performance evaluation process,' she says, 'requires that supervisors and employees jointly set clear performance objectives, including:

■ Identifying the specific tasks and behaviours as objectives to be accomplished during a performance cycle

■ Establishing how to measure the objectives

■ Prioritizing work by identifying those results most crucial and those that can be deferred

■ Analysing how objectives support group work goals.'

Fay suggests that managers also include three other areas as part of the overall assessment process. 'Supervisors should define tasks as much as possible in terms of output,' she believes. 'Having measurable results and – if possible – milestones built into the job makes remote supervising much easier. Supervisors of teleworkers must focus on the employee's expected work product. Frequent communication between the supervisor and the teleworker is important to ensure that tasks and performance expectations are clearly defined. Electronic and voice-mail access for the teleworker facilitates daily contact with the supervisor and other personnel.' Fay also advises that 'Accessibility is an important issue. Teleworkers should be easy to reach within a certain amount of time. On the other hand, supervisors should accept that employees, whether teleworking or on-site, may not always be readily accessible. However, all organizational policies regarding attendance and hours worked should also apply to teleworking employees. The teleworker and his or her supervisor should agree upon the schedule of regular work hours. This is important for the purpose of defining the teleworker's job period. Unless a different work schedule is designated, teleworker's hours are assumed to be, say from 08.00 to 17.00, Monday to Friday, with a one-hour meal break that is considered "off-duty" time. Any changes of work hours, or work location, should be reviewed and approved by the supervisor in advance.

Union views on telework

A number of trade unions both in Europe and the USA are viewing the advent of telework as a danger, both to their power position and as a potential way of changing the employment conditions of their members. Bill Walsh, the national officer of MSF, has drawn up a fourteen-point checklist that he recommends for employees negotiating home-based teleworking arrangements. It is a useful example of what employers with unionized employees might expect to see as a starting point for bargaining – so stay aware of it:

■ Home-based working should always be voluntary.
■ Home-based workers should be employees (enjoying full employment rights) and not self-employed sub-contractors.
■ Ideally, home-based teleworking should operate from a separate room in the home, properly examined by qualified health and safety experts to ensure a safe working environment.
■ There should be regular opportunities for teleworkers in the same organization to meet each other, as well as

non-teleworking colleagues and managers, so that people do not feel isolated or excluded.

■ Teleworkers should have access to electronic mail and telephone links with each other – using the scope of the technology to expand contact between people.

■ Each teleworker should be assigned a particular manager, whose responsibility it should be to keep in regular contact and who would also meet the teleworker on a regular basis.

■ Teleworkers should enjoy the same rates of pay and other employment benefits as non-teleworking employees in an organization.

■ Teleworkers should be included in the career development programme of the organization in which they work.

■ All the equipment used should be supplied and maintained by the employer.

■ Financial arrangements should be agreed to cover the extra costs of teleworking, such as heating, lighting, etc., and it may also be appropriate for a rental agreement to be agreed for the use the employer makes of the employee's home.

■ Employers should be responsible for the health and safety of teleworkers and have specialist health and safety advisers to give advice and regularly visit and monitor health and safety.

■ Teleworkers should be represented, through their own employee representatives, on health and safety committees of the organizations that employ them.

■ Teleworkers should enjoy the same rights as other workers, to join trade unions and should have access to representatives, including the right to elect their own. In this regard, trade unions will need to think about the services they made need to offer teleworkers, including access to electronic mail, notice-boards, etc.

■ Employees who transfer from conventional working to home-based teleworking should be entitled to a trial period and should have the right to return to the previous arrangements. All teleworkers should be entitled to an annual review of the arrangements and have a right to revert to the previous employment arrangement if they so wish.

Look around your office. How many people spend large amounts of time on the phone? Probably a great number, because that's what you pay them to do – right? So, if they can organize their internal meetings on two days each week, why don't they spend the rest of the time at home, or in a local service centre close to their homes making the same calls?

What is noticeable in telework development is that individual companies use a basic, standard formula for setting up the process and then add on items that meet their own needs and organizational culture. For example, AT&T has implemented successful telework programmes over a number of years and their advice to supervisors and managers getting involved in this area shows that they not only recognize teleworking as a valuable method of working but also see it as part of a work revolution. Here's some advice AT&T give to teleworker's supervisors.

A challenge to management traditions

'Teleworking challenges management traditions. It means a significant change in how we think about work and supervising employees. Teleworking moves the work to wherever the people are giving the term "office" new meaning. It means breaking away from the idea that supervisors have to remain in a central location and manage by observation. Teleworking strongly brings forth the issues of employee trust and empowerment. It also brings up supervisory challenges to keep teleworkers an integral part of the office team.' Their advice adds, 'Don't assume however that you don't have the right tools for teleworking. You do. Existing supervisory skills translate well when overseeing teleworkers. Basic management skills are just as important for teleworkers as they are for people in the office. But you may need to tailor your supervision for those working at home by focusing more on results and less on observing your employees hard at work.'

Two- or three-day-a-week teleworkers need to be organized. One supervisor reports that a member of his staff had to work two hours later each night before his telework days to copy and pack everything he needed to work at home.

AT&T also offer some other smart tips not completely covered by others:

- Use planning skills to effectively distribute work so that in-office personnel and teleworkers are treated equally.

- Make the most of time spent with remote workers to coach and develop the teleworker's capabilities. Quickly enforce positive behaviour and bring unsatisfactory performance to the employee's attention.

Don't overlook the office-bound employees either

Assuming that finally the teleworkers are operational, there is one other issue that needs to be taken into consideration. What happens to the office-bound employees left behind? Well, in most cases, companies have taken it upon themselves to do four things:

- Make sure that non-teleworkers are fully aware of the scheme and how it works, including the rules and regulations.
- If someone wasn't chosen because they were not regarded as an ideal teleworker, explain that and set in motion appropriate training that may be able to change this situation.
- Make certain that non-teleworkers don't get stuck with office work that used to be done by the teleworker.
- Impress upon everyone that this is a team and success is dependent on the whole group, teleworker and non-teleworker alike.

Don't alienate the ones left behind at head office and make it clear that their positions aren't up for grabs, or that they'll all have to telework eventually. In this new working world, people need to feel they have security as well as opportunity.

They shall not telework

Another way of looking at the telework process and how to make it successful – this assumes that somewhere along the line your organization is going to take the plunge and do it – is to take the opposing approach. Who don't you want to telework? Often getting that answered as early in the process as possible can save a lot of problems later on. Managers report that when the concept of telework is first mooted it is quite often the most unsuitable candidates who step up smartly and volunteer. The others who do are the really smart ones, who in your heart of hearts you'd rather have sticking around the office! Therefore, it needs to be made clear from the outset what the standards are and the type of people and skills that will qualify. Anyone who thinks that this is an opportunity to get up late and catch up on the work later is obviously not a serious candidate. Neither is it a way to

According to media research, a job advertised with the option of teleworking can attract six times as many responses.

banish or exile difficult employees you haven't the nerve to fire or those you cannot persuade anyone else to take onto their team.

Teleworking isn't as much fun as it sounds. There are literally a thousand-and-one possible distractions that can shake-up the work pattern of even the most stoical and dedicated teleworker. Experts suggest that it can take up to six months – and certainly three – for teleworkers to settle into a really regular, comfortable routine. Although this might seem to belie the fact that in the first months productivity gains are often highest, it is usually because – wanting to impress – the newly commissioned teleworker wants to make a good impression whatever the trials and tribulations they may be suffering.

Telecommunications company BT have recorded a few of the difficulties teleworkers report:

- Loss of office social life
- Loss of colleagues' expertise
- 'Trapped' at home 24 hours a day
- Reduced training opportunities
- Reduced information input
- Reduced promotion opportunities
- Noisy, intrusive, family or partner

- Reduced confidentiality of work
- Reduced equipment facilities
- Intrusive neighbours and friends
- Poor office accommodation
- Difficulty with work routine
- Inadequate space for meetings
- Time-wasting trivia

These are just some of the difficulties being reported to managers and supervisors the world over every day of the working week. The trouble is, for a lot of employees the first thing that comes to mind when teleworking is mentioned is 'I get to stay at home two or three days a week'. But it is by no means a way to escape office routine. On the contrary, telework can involve **a lot more hard work**, dedication and the inevitable adjustment.

Overcoming 'cabin fever'

The biggest down of all, even for the most organized and enthusiastic teleworker, is the feeling dubbed 'cabin fever.' Even the occasional phone call from a co-worker doesn't totally relieve the feeling that you are really on your own. Teleworkers left without face-to-face contact for too long –

especially in the early stages – do get a mild paranoia about the step they have taken and whether it will affect their futures. The antidote is to make certain that they do get to the old office site as often as possible and spend time with colleagues. Many workers don't realize it, but the sandwich around the corner, the coffee or glass of wine after work, are key parts of their day.

June Langhoff, author of Telecom Made Easy, agrees and adds several other categories of disillusioned teleworker that need attention. 'Teleworking has its negative aspects,' she says. 'it's certainly not for everybody. Isolation and procrastination – even boredom – get to some. Because the office can be anywhere they park their lap-top, workaholics often find it difficult to end their day. In other cases, temptations such as a much-too-handy refrigerator, neighbours who think that work-at-homers aren't really working, household chores and family distractions can easily undermine others.'

Horror stories of the home commute

Collecting horror stories from its staff of home-worker horrors has become something of an obsession at BT – the UK telecommunications group. They even publish some of them in their brochures!

Here's BT's communications department's thoughts on teleworking from home; quite likely to put anyone off forever. According to BT, 'Some teleworkers tell a different tale of family interactions with their work. Partners have rows and some partners may decide to take revenge on the hapless teleworker just as they are talking by phone to their boss or best customer. There are tales of vital meetings being sabotaged by irate spouses who feel their personal space is being invaded. Spilling coffee in the laps of important visitors; laying used nappies like bear traps on the route to the only toilet, which has no toilet rolls; blocking in the visitors' cars before leaving for the day with the only keys or, a sad but true tale, walking calmly into the meeting and emptying a huge bowl of cold water over one's spouse before calmly and silently walking out again!'

Distractions can come in a variety of shapes, sizes and disguises. Teleworkers report that until they stayed at home from Monday to Friday they had no idea just what went on in their neighbourhood. Mail delivery, special delivery by courier services and catalogue firms, passing sales people, market researchers, gardeners and a hundred others all beat a path to the door.

Distractions aside, other telework beginners report that they often have problems settling down to work, but once they get going they find it equally as difficult to stop. At the office it's easy, there are routines throughout the day that structure your time for you, so you often don't think about them at all. At home it is different and simply putting in more hours to get something done isn't a good idea, because a tired and worried teleworker is just as unproductive as a tired and worried office worker.

One way to get around overwork – or not getting started – is to set strict business hours and stick to them. Let your supervisor and your co-workers know what these hours are so they will know when they can call you at home. Also, even though you are working at home, you don't have to respond to every work request immediately – you wouldn't if you were back in the office, would you ? Respond to urgent requests as quickly as you can but keep others for later, when you have finished other assigned tasks. Above all, make sure you create and stick to these routines and don't get put upon to do extra work, just because others back at the office think you have time on your hands.

While you are establishing those rules about your work day, make sure your family or partner knows them – and respects them – as well. Print them out and stick them on your 'office' door and make it clear you are not to be disturbed. This is very important indeed!

Making it clear to your spouse or partner exactly what you are doing is paramount. Often they won't really know much about your work and what you do. Finding out can come as a shock – especially if you are taking over parts of the home you share. Norwegian consultant John Bakke calls it the moment that 'the home becomes a machine for working in'. He advises that when 'the norms and expectations for social life at home are challenged it does seem necessary to establish an etiquette for teleworking on the domestic scene, regarding the division between work and leisure – a sensible, delicate Norwegian way of saying, "stay out of my space until six – or else!"'

Are your reasons for teleworking the right ones?

Julia Gosling, editor of Flexible Working magazine in the UK adds another few potential dangers of her own that would-be teleworkers need to watch out for. She believes that 'the disadvantages for employees are many and are often overlooked by employers wanting to cut costs'. One of her major concerns for teleworkers is 'the inability to draw the line between home and work (for example, working into the night), which can result in domestic tensions' as well as 'the effect of cultural change. An unsupported move into a completely new routine and environment can be damaging.'

Assign an advocate or, better still, a team to handle any disputes and problems that arise from teleworking. A representative from management, unions, staff, human resources and information systems makes an excellent group.

Focusing her attention on telework as an opportunity for the unscrupulous employer to get one over on the teleworker, Gosling says that she is also worried about the 'potential for a gradual disintegration of employee rights as the "self-employed" ethic becomes more prevalent. This means needing to allow for traditional company benefits such as private health care, pensions, sick pay, holiday pay and maternity leave.'

Employers featured in this book are of the caring kind that Gosling would approve. All the same, trying to put a lid on overall cost spirals can create the potential for changes in worker protection that employees need to be on guard against.

Much of the home part of telework is sheer common sense. With the right preparation and the right planning settling into a routine can be achieved.

Never agree to telework just to keep employees happy. Make sure that this is a win–win situation, for the organization and for the individual.

Certainly, results from across Europe and from the USA – where the process is far more advanced in penetration and number of teleworkers – show that once companies have got over their initial concerns and learned to manage remote workers the benefits can be legion. All that remains, is for more of us to take the plunge and try it !

Executive summary

- Telework centres require that you shop carefully and look to future as well as immediate requirements.

- Telework may not be a winner with trade unions but they do have their manifesto of what it should cover.

- Telework is a mystery to a lot of middle-aged managers.

- Telework supervision requires a new style of manager to get the most out of it.

- Telework entails a move from being a leader to being a coordinator.

- Telework calls on skills that most of us possess.

- Telework isn't always as much fun as it sounds – it takes dedication and determination.

6 Examining the telework debate so far

Telework is an enigma – embraced by some, misunderstood by many. It is a child of the twenty-first century that has had a premature birth. No one is quite sure who or what is driving telework as a concept.

- In the USA state and national governments are legislating for it as part of clean air acts and getting commuters off the streets and freeways.
- Employers are looking to it as a way to cut costs, boost productivity and trim expensive headquarter staffs.
- In-the-know individuals, entrepreneurs and smart companies are using it as a ticket to a new workstyle.

So what does this leave us with?

First, this book is not about telework but about part of a revolution that allows us to do our work differently. All of us should accept by now that the world of work is changing, and that there is precious little individuals or organizations can do to stop the tidal wave of change taking place all around us. Until now, many commentators – ignoring much of what was becoming daily more practicable and possible through technology – talked about business centres. It wasn't Germany or Britain or Spain that was attracting jobs and services – it was places. For example, companies and government workers migrate to Brussels, because it is a centre and there are a large supply of skilled, multi-lingual, well-educated people. Those people don't live in Belgium, they live in an international society where the postmark just happens to be Brussels. Similarly, bankers and financiers live in London, not England, and Asian and Western companies congregate in Tokyo, Singapore and Hong Kong, because it is – up until now – the place that counts.

in brief. 'Because of the accumulated impacts of technology development, we have entered an age of plenty – without really recognizing it. But for some unfathomable reasons we insist on approaching the challenges before us as if we were paupers.'
– Eric Britton

Then along comes teleworking and changes the equation – or, for the present, begins to change the equation. Here's an example. The European president of a US industrial firm lives on the outskirts of Brussels. He has been there with his wife and two children for two years, and they have never been into the centre of town. Each morning he travels to work by car to an office complex close to the airport and it takes him 15 minutes. His wife drives the children to an American school 15 minutes in the other direction. Most months he is out of the country for at least twelve working days. Other times, he talks constantly on the phone and uses his e-mail wherever he is. He is one of an increasing number of new-style managers that have an almost virtual headquarters (there are eight people in total). Every task and project is

106

farmed out to the divisional subsidiaries, which are no longer organized by country but by the businesses they are in and the centres of excellence they control. Apart from the charming foreign accent of his assistant, this man could be in Deerfield outside Chicago.

But the significant fact is that he is using modern communications to a level that has not been seen before by senior managers. He is making it work for himself and for his organization – his office and the offices of his managers are wherever the lap-top is.

In case you don't know, there are now thousands of these people – probably hundreds of thousands already in a new working world. Conversely, in downtown Brussels there is a manager of the same age with practically the same responsibilities who is still dictating to his secretary every morning after a 90-minute commute in close to grid-locked traffic.

Take these two very different people, these two opposed management styles, and consider just how different they are. But also consider that if all of us as managers don't get more like manager number one, we are not going to survive. As others begin to embrace the technology that makes each of us able to take instant, individual action we will not get left behind, we will literally disappear. And if our own senior management do not have an honest, in-depth understanding of what telematics can do today and is likely to achieve tomorrow, our organizations are going to vanish faster than we would ever have thought possible.

But the sense of place issue – of being where the action is – is going to go through an even bigger revolution. It might take some time, but as technology speeds up and as it brings more power, more opportunity to the individual, we won't need to get together every day to meet our business obligations. Certainly, face-to-face meetings will always be necessary, a video call will never replace being in the same room as someone else, but those meetings won't have to be so frequent.

So, those of us who have access to the technology, know how to use it effectively and adapt it to our personal needs won't have to be in Brussels or New York or Berlin every day – nether will many of the staff.

Do you need a headquarters at all?

Consider this. If you had no headquarters, or a very small central office, you could get together with all your senior people twice a month anywhere you wanted (airport business centres are increasingly popular) and the travel costs would be more than paid for in the savings on office costs. Certainly as more and more companies benefit from the creation of multi-cultural/multi-country project teams, or business practice-based cross-border workgroups, getting together in a location that fits the needs of the group is more important than going to a country office each day.

For every dollar spent on teleworking at AT&T, two dollars were saved. The reduction in office space was the key.

But the drive for more productivity and more new ideas, coupled to already available technology, is going to change the emphasis on where – which – places people will want to be, when a lot more managers wake up to not virtual reality, but real reality. Few people will stay in rainy, high-taxed Brussels if they don't have to go to an office each day. Why sit in the snows of Chicago if you can do it in Miami?

Where would you run your company from?

So what's the prediction? Let's try Florida, let's try southern Spain, the south of France. Let's try anywhere that has modern, cheap, reliable teleservices and a good transport infrastructure (the ability to fly to places, quickly, easily and inexpensively). Hard to believe? It's already happening.

The marketing vice-president of a large European manufacturer spends nine months of his year in Marbella, southern Spain. His marketing team is widely dispersed across Europe, and they come together for two or three days at present every two weeks in a different location. The rest is driven by phone, e-mail and fax (a few years ago in a bid to encourage just this sort of inward investment, Spain cut its international telecom tariffs by 50 per cent). From two local airports (Malaga and Gibraltar), he can fly to London – the hub for Europe – at least twelve times each day. If he leaves his home at eight in the morning he can have an early dinner in New York. The autopistas are relatively uncrowded – despite the other estimated 100 000 similar 'new arrivals' – and the airport is modern with excellent business facilities if there is any delay.

From skier's paradise to an Internet junkie's hide-away, Teluride, Colorado, has shown just what you can do when you take telework as a serious option to change your local economy. With funds to purchase and install a high-performance server, Teluride workers can now send data around the world for the cost of a local phone call. Today more than one-third of the village's 1500 residents have Internet access, compared to an average of less than five per cent nationally.

A major work revolution

What we are seeing is a revolution that is not only for senior businessmen but also for all the specialists that they employ as well. There will be – in most cases – a hard-core staff to make the process work, but a great deal of that is going to be outsourced to cover centralized leasing on phone lines, equipment, travel buying and so on.

There is already a revolution as companies seek more and more ways to reduce costs and improve return to shareholders. Telework is going to spur the revolution, the move to a new working world, even faster than we thought possible.

In forecasting the future some have said that the USA will win. Less costly infrastructure, cheaper products and a more pioneering attitude will give America the telework/telecommute lead and push them into the winner's circle. But don't be too sure. One of the things that telework relies on is the ability for individuals to rely on a solid home-based social structure to replace the social interaction of the office. Much of Europe – the southern part at least – and most of Asia relies on the family, not the firm, to be there for them in times of need. Assuming they can get access and afford the technology – something all the surveys say they don't have yet – these nations could be candidates for being super-teleworkers.

Of course, what telework in the business sense will also do is increase global business dealing and that will also mean – since much of the software is controlled and developed by the USA – that English will dominate a great deal of telework opportunities. Local language help-desks might be staffed by remote-workers, but chances are that they will be more likely to hold down the job if they can help out in English as well as their own language.

The dangers inherent in this technical revolution that will prompt ever faster changes to new working styles is that it will disenfranchise not only large parts of the world that cannot afford it but also lots of people who were brought up with the wrong type of training (many schools are still teaching children ways to look at the world that are totally out of keeping with current reality), and this is already beginning to have an alienating effect.

So look for government action to take place when they discover how huge the revolution is. Expect and plan for a trade union backlash as jobs slip away to lower bidders, and specialists and managers become teleworkers as well.

Is there really any way back?

Many of the examples used in this book make an interesting point in their telework manuals and commentators and telework gurus mention it as well: 'If you don't like telework, come back and work in the traditional office.' What a lovely, altruistic idea! Sadly, it is completely wrong-headed. Although there may be a few cases in the great scheme of things where this happens, in the most part telework is part of a planned reduction of office-bound staff. It is part of creating greater flexibility, it is shaking out overheads. Few companies contemplating telework programmes are going to reverse the process – they are much more likely to increase it. And as technology costs tumble and infrastructure improves, telework is going to be the way most of us do our day-to-day jobs. Sure, there will be managers, but they will be composites of the executives we know today, multi-skilled

for a multi-task environment. The other factor that has to be built into that is the increasing number of specialists that are either happy where they are – and won't move to a new job but will telework – or have other work/life plans. Offering the right telework and travel-based package to these people can help secure valuable talent – it can also help secure and retain workers who might otherwise leave for the competition.

In the first ever mass-media teleworking advertising campaign, a Pacific Bell spokesperson halts Californian freeway traffic with a loud-hailer and police-style barricades and succeeds in his mission to send office-bound commuters home to work.

This paints a picture that can be looked on as either packed with the primary colours of opportunity or awash with the pastel greys and browns of organizations and individuals trapped in a past way of work. Nothing, of course, is that simple. With reduced commuting to offices in our towns and cities, depressed inner-city areas may blossom once more. Telework doesn't have to be work done in a cottage with roses around the door, far from it. Properly promoted it can bring economic prosperity to anyone on the end of a fibre-optic cable.

Think of telework as a complete work revolution that, yes, brings the work to the worker but also offers a kaleidoscope of opportunities for everyone who has to work for a living. It frees all of us, chief executive, salesperson, clerical worker, designer, programmer, to create work the way we want it to be. Far from fearing it, we should, sensibly, embrace what it can offer each and every one of us.

Telework, management's slow discovery

Julia Gosling, the editor of Flexible Working magazine, agrees that management still have some way to go in understanding what telework means as a business revolution. 'I think that teleworking and others forms of remote work will increase over the next five years,' she says, 'and this will be a combination of environmental pressures and cost-cutting initiatives from employers.'

But Gosling – like other close observers of the teleworking scene – is sure that managers have yet to see its full potential. 'Very few employers are currently far-sighted enough to see the many advantages that can come from a well-managed flexible working strategy. Too many of them see it as an easy way to reduce overheads, rather than an opportunity to increase productivity.' She adds, 'Investments need to be made in training personnel managers and other key staff to manage remote workers effectively or many of the potential benefits will be lost.' Telework consultant Gil Gordon concurs: 'Despite a lack of senior management direction and vision, we'll continue to see office workers increase their use of teleworking as long as their employers are open-minded and understand the business benefits.'

Whether employers really will understand the total benefits to teleworkers is doubted by Julia Gosling, who worries that they – certainly at present – see it as an opportunity to reduce the responsibility they have for their employees. Because of that, Gosling predicts that there 'will be a backlash against organizations "divesting" themselves of responsibility for their employees, by downsizing and then re-employing personnel and consultants and freelancers.' She adds, 'There will need to be major developments in employment law and policy to maintain employee rights.'

Jack Nilles – one of telework's greatest advocates – sees employers sticking to their telework plans despite some of the disadvantages, which he lists as:

- The need to invest in more and more telecommunications technology
- The need to increase information security provisions
- The possible upcoming conflicts with unions
- The need for increased management training
- The fear (usually unjustified) of decreased employee interaction – especially in teams.

One point to keep very much on top of the mind in planning any telework experiment or permanent set up: check out access to Internet links. All those ads that say send your messages around the world for the cost of a local call may be true in some places, in others it's a parent's phone bill horror-story. Large pieces of the US and much of Europe are not a local call but a long-distance call away to connect to Internet servers. For example, in Belgium, the only Compuserve link at time of writing was Brussels; in Spain it's Barcelona or Madrid and so on. A teleworker with heavy on-line usage can find it very expensive very quickly if they are in an isolated rural location.

Nilles is not alone in his concerns. In the USA a nationwide interagency telecommuting initiative raised some of the key worries cited by both government departments and private enterprise in the successful application of teleworking to their operations:

■ Cost of technology initially and in the future
■ Geographical and cultural availability – and access – to the technology
■ User-friendliness of the technology and software computability
■ Ease of establishing data link-ups from remote locations
■ Telecommunication incompatibilities and cost of line charges
■ Effective use of interactive video technology
■ Credible data security

All these are crucial areas that, if you imagine they are having a hard time resolving in the USA, are going to concentrate many business brains in Europe over the next several years, or decades depending on your level of optimism or pessimism.

With the possibility of data literally flying around all over the place, security is an issue. Therefore, set a security standard and stick to it.

The trek to a new world of work

Eric Britton, a consultant with EcoPlan in Paris, says that we should think of what's happening to our working lives as 'a migration, with an entire population trooping from an exhausted countryside to new and fertile valleys. Each year we are going to see a growing number of people migrating to the new forms of work which are going to be oriented not to jobs, but careers, not to single employer skills, not to subservience to a single master but networks of associates and clients.' But, according to Britton, management hasn't recognized the opportunities inherent in the whole colourful picture yet. 'All of this is moving and changing very fast – certainly much faster than those of us who do not have time to follow these developments carefully will be aware. In fact the pace of development is even faster than many of the enthusiastic tele-philes may imagine.' He adds, 'As important as sheer technology advance, however, will be the development of the adaptive capacities of those groups (organizations and managers) and institutions who learn how to put these opportunities to work.' Forecasting that 'the transition to telework is going to take place with or without the benefit of guiding government policy' – much of which is still based on the old work-mode of a permanent, full-time job, with a single employer in one (distant) place – Britton says that 'telework is a concept that needs to be carefully interpreted from two very different aspects. On the one hand, it refers to a broad package of technologies and associated working arrangements – this is what most discussions on these matters tends to emphasize. But telework has another role as well: that of an enabler, something that can help us to think creatively about new ways to work in the broadest sense.'

Beware of telework programmes that are driven by human resource considerations alone. Telework today is the successful marriage of people *and* technology – don't have one without the other.

It may sound obvious, but experience shows it's not! Check compatibility of the teleworkers equipment with that of the system they will work through. No two computers ever seem to be configured totally alike.

A report by MTA concurs, 'Telework, teletrade and open electronic networking present immense economic and work opportunities,' they say, 'but few of these opportunities will be in old-style jobs with old-style companies doing old-style things. The new environment calls for individuals to be more inventive and creative in their approach to business and work. This must be matched by governments at all levels making special efforts to ensure that natural inertia doesn't sustain market's focus on supporting old-style employers and old-style employees at the expense of stifling innovators.' MTA go on to warn that 'this doesn't mean we should forget the many people whose education, upbringing and experience has fitted them only for old-style paid employment in old-style jobs, and hasn't at all prepared them for generating their own work opportunities or taking a creative or self-managed approach to paid work.' MTA see that 'these people need a lot of help during the transition from a society built around paid employment to one sustained by creativity and work opportunities. What's important is that we provide this help in ways that makes it easier for them to change and develop, not in ways that seek to protect them from change.' They conclude, 'If we take a defensive, protective approach, the effect will be to hold back the innovators and those who are at the forefront of change, whom we rely on for our future prosperity: and it won't help the disadvantaged either. It will simply reinforce the gap between the new modes and the old.'

Projections estimate that by the year 2000, one in every three US workers will be working from a home office full- or part-time.

Getting the chief executive on board

Management – and a lot of senior managers at that – seem to be one of the stumbling blocks to creating telework as a viable alternative to office-based jobs – an oversight based on ignorance, rather than a deliberate decision it would seem. Dr R. Grant Tate, president of the Bridgewater Group, a globally networked consulting firm operating out of the Netherlands, feels that we should look to a new type of chief executive officer (CEO) if we are to fully take on board these new technologies and the advantages they can create. Says Tate, 'executives are relatively invisible on both internal and external networks. I call them "cold" nodes. Sure, occasionally Microsoft's Bill Gates or another CEO of a large knowledge-based company may participate in on-line interviews, but inside most networked companies, top executives remain isolated and inaccessible – they are cold nodes.' He goes on, 'these executives think that e-mail and other network features are the tools of the workers – on a par with the machine tools of bygone days, or they might say that computers and networks are the domain of the "techies" and have no place in the executive suite. Some executives are afraid to expose their lack of computer – or even typing – skills, while others may fear the consequences of opening themselves to questioning by their employees, still others – who might well appreciate the convenience of e-mail – let their secretary be the interface to the network. These executives,' thinks Tate, 'are shirking their responsibility for leadership – and missing a major opportunity to reform their organizations.' He believes that 'the networked world demands new leadership methods'.

Creating telework systems is not like creating an in-company IT network. Take care! Make sure your IT professional really knows something about telework before you let them loose on a project.

Enter the hot node executive

'Inspirational leaders set the tone for their organizations,' says Tate. 'An executive who participates in the company's network can set a positive example for the whole organization – people will feel closer to an executive who is a "hot" node.' He adds, 'the hot node executive can feel the pulse of his or her team by seeing how employees use the network and by observing the expression and quality of the messages and information. Smart executives use the company's network to open up new channels of communication with their employees. Hot node executives know the capabilities of the network and use them!' Tate says that a true hot node executive can make a great impact on the organization without leaving his or her office – or home – chair. 'They make sure that everyone knows about the company goals and performance via the network. Important company information is available on-line. Company news is flashed to everyone as soon as it happens. The CEO is often available for on-line discussions and questions – and everyone knows the top executives' e-mail addresses.' Even in a

networked society, Tate is sure that 'Great leaders keep a strong sense of humanity in their organizations. They understand the technology, but they know how to keep it in perspective. They encourage others to be sensitive to good human relations, to care about each other and to give top service to customers. As executives,' he concludes, 'we have a deep responsibility to influence the direction of the networked society. We are all citizens of the global village.'

Scenarios for teleworking's future

Tony Hodgson is a scenario planner, who has teleworked himself from the noise and grime of London to a hillside home in Perthshire, Scotland. During his career he has worked with Shell, Hewlett-Packard and British Telecom (BT) among others in developing business scenario strategies. Here are Hodgson's four scenarios of where teleworking and its attendant technology could take us in the future.

First of all he warns us that scenarios:

■ Are not predictions but futures imagined on the basis of different sets of assumptions
■ Their value is in challenging the assumptions of our default scenario, that is, the one we *currently* believe and bet on
■ Their value is that experience shows that our default scenarios are usually wrong
■ The scenarios also have value in provoking us to think of new options that can be useful however the future turns out

THE FOUR SCENARIOS

Scenario One: Jewels in a dark maze

Despite the heralding of the New World Order, ethnic tensions continue to fragment the planet and inhibit the creation of wealth, in terms of both economics and well-being. In conflict zones fragile peace processes keep breaking down to be precariously reformed. The borderless world, therefore, is a reality only for the wealthy few, creating a two-speed society where local markets are still fairly diverse and fragmented. The global multinationals find the crucial competence for survival shifts from downsizing and re-engineering to political savvy and the ability to present many faces to many communities. Although the 'wired world' is important, where global coherence is possible the accent is on being perceived as locally customized. There are zones of high value and achievement but they are found and entered with difficulty in complex webs of protective interest.

Impact on teleworking:

- Tends to be very culturally divergent
- Unevenly taken up as ethnic customs prevail
- Organizations use it intensively at international management level but the uptake locally is uneven

Scenario Two: A learning renaissance?

The much-hyped promise of multi-media and the interactive world is never quite delivered, somewhat reminiscent of the promises made for programs learning in the 1960s. The value of the printed page is still preferred over the screen as a basic medium of recording and studying knowledge, with its freedom to annotate. Driving forces in education take up research findings that the human brain is really connected to the senses and the 'virtual world', although superior in some aspects, falls far short of an adequate stimulation to the development of intelligence. The working environments of people begin to subsume the use of the computer and the screen to that of the telephone as a background utility for the more serious and enjoyable occupation of human face-to-face interaction.

Impact on teleworking :

- Teleworking tends to remain relatively conventional with emphasis on the transmission of documents with printing and scanning primary interface tools
- Teleworking does not become the preferred method of serious education
- Teleworking probably becomes more the new equivalent of 'manual worker'; the more intelligent work is still done by face to face and paper

Scenario Three: Everywhere new communities

The impact of the convergence of telecoms, the Internet and Web, and interactive TV with high bandwidth continue an exponential growth of communication between 'plugged-in people' wherever they are. Governments attempting to control access and content largely fail and the breakdown of nationalism and the nation state is replaced by the economics of regions. These are of two types: physical regions based around vibrant 'city state' economies and virtual regions based around globally networked common interests. The nature of society at all levels goes through a major paradigm shift in which, after a period of seeming breakdown in traditional mores, new values emerge which are more open and less bigoted than the present world.

Impact on teleworking:

■ For many of the new communities the teleconnection is a crucial linking factor in developing their new identities
■ The global network is a prime carrier of the new virtual communities
■ However, regional economics determine that people proximity is still the major driving force in establishing productive alliances

Scenario Four: The visualate society:

The global information highway becomes the key to communication in a rising generation (today often called the 'Nintendo' generation) whose intelligence and intellectual processes are based on visual and time-based media, rather than the literate and numerate paradigm of the last 2000 years. Contrary to the sceptics, substantial intellectual and practical achievement emerges from these new ways of thinking and relating. The shift is from a left-brained bureaucracy to a right-brained meritocracy. People unable to enter this new world are increasingly considered inadequate or antiques. New ways of practising and creating art, science and management evolve which are not necessarily much better than the old ways but are certainly cast in a new medium.

Impact on teleworking :

- This is really a *super* teleworking scenario where the primary intellectual and decision-making power of the world is channelled through complex multimedia channels
- The skills of teleworking transform from traditional methods put in electronic form (e-mail) to quite new ways of working in and over the media. These methods are centred on the validity of visual thinking
- The e-mail type of transactions become what the less able and privileged majority have to use

TURNING POINTS BETWEEN THE SCENARIOS

Although life is more complicated than clear unambiguous division, it can be helpful to distinguish *turning points* which may indicate that one scenario rather than another may become a dominant feature of the future. The turning points are indicated in Figure 6.1 by circles. The first hinges on the question as to whether the promises of the technologically networked world is hype or for real. If it is hype, then the future may depend on a second turning point as to whether the forces of conflict or the force of educational renewal prevail. If the networked world is for real then will the much-vaunted high bandwidth emerge as effective and with substance or will it remain as entertainment for the masses and decision makers stick to human contact and paperwork? However, each person will possibly see other ways of distinguishing between futures.

All citizens of a global village perhaps, but one that has its bad sides and good sides, one where you can be lucky and be born on the right side of the technology tracks. The telework debate will go on, but while it is being debated organizations and institutions will be finding their own ways to tackle it and wring the most out of it.

It's been estimated that if only five per cent of the commuters in Los Angeles County teleworked just one day a week they would eliminate 205 million miles driven and keep 47 000 tons of pollutants from entering the atmosphere each year.

At its best it will give new freedoms to many of us to realize and a new world of work. Let us hope that this new world of work, this new fertile valley, has room for the vast

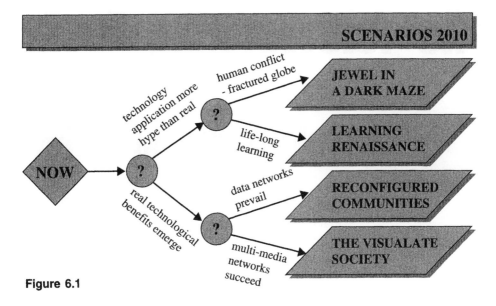

SCENARIOS 2010

technology application more hype than real

human conflict - fractured globe

JEWEL IN A DARK MAZE

life-long learning

LEARNING RENAISSANCE

NOW

real technological benefits emerge

data networks prevail

RECONFIGURED COMMUNITIES

multi-media networks succeed

THE VISUALATE SOCIETY

Figure 6.1

majority of us inside it. Properly managed, properly understood by our 'digitally homeless', we might have a chance.

Executive summary

■ Telework shouldn't just be a way to cut costs, but a lot of employers see it that way: beware a backlash from governments and unions.

■ Telework gives tremendous new career freedoms to those who know how to take advantage of it.

■ Teleworking is a key part of moving to a whole new world of work for many of us.

■ Telework needs new concepts, new business methods and ideas to thrive.

■ Telework still has downsides: costs of equipment and plug-in-ability are just two.

■ Telework can be used to advantage by smart CEOs to build a new corporate consensus and culture.

The Teleworking Toolkit

Telework guidelines

This is practical, straightforward set of telework guidelines that can be easily adapted to any business or work situation.

United States Office of Personnel Management – Sample Agreement Between Agency and Employee Approved for Telecommuting on a Continuing Basis

The supervisor and the employees should keep a copy of the agreement for reference.

Voluntary Participation

Employee voluntarily agrees to work at the agency-approved alternative workplace indicated below and to follow all applicable policies and procedures. Employee recognizes that the telecommuting arrangement is not an employee benefit but an additional method the agency may approve to accomplish work.

Trial Period

Employee and agency agree to try out the arrangement for at least [specify number] months unless unforeseeable difficulties require earlier cancellation.

Salary and Benefits

Agency agrees that a telecommuting arrangement is not a basis for changing the employee's salary or benefits.

Duty Station and Alternative Workplace

Agency and employee agree that the employee's official duty station is [indicate duty station for regular office] and that the employee's approved alternative workplace is: [specify street and number, city and state].

Note: All pay, leave, and travel entitlements are based on the official duty station.

Telework guidelines

Official Duties

Unless otherwise instructed, employee agrees to perform official duties only at the regular office or agency approved-alternative workplace. Employee agrees not to conduct personal business while in official duty status at the alternative workplace, for example, caring for dependents or making home repairs.

Work Schedule and Tour of Duty

Agency and employee agree the employee's official tour of duty will be: [specify days, hours, and location, i.e. the regular office or the alternative workplace].

Time and Attendance

Agency agrees to make sure the telecommuting employee's timekeeper has a copy of the employee's work schedule. The supervisor agrees to certify biweekly the time and attendance for hours worked at the regular office and the alternative workplace. (Note: agency may require employee to complete self-certification form.)

Leave

Employee agrees to follow established office procedures for requesting and obtaining approval of leave.

Overtime

Employee agrees to work overtime only when ordered and approved by the supervisor in advance and understands that working overtime without such approval may result in termination of the telecommuting privilege and/or other appropriate action.

Equipment/Supplies

Employee agrees to protect any Government-owned equipment and to use the equipment only for official purposes. The agency agrees to install, service, and maintain any Government-owned equipment issued to the telecommuting employee. The employee agrees to install, service, and maintain any personal equipment used. The agency agrees to provide the employee with all necessary office supplies and also reimburse the employee for business-related long distance telephone calls.

Security

If the Government provides computer equipment for the alternative workplace, employee agrees to the following security provisions: [insert agency-specific language].

Liability

The employee understands that the Government will not be liable for damages to all employee's personal or real property while the employee is working at the approved alternative workplace, except to the extent the Government is held liable by the Federal Tort Claims Act or the Military Personnel and Civilian Employees Claims Act.

Work Area

The employee agrees to provide a work area adequate for performance of official duties.

Worksite Inspection

The employee agrees to permit the Government to inspect the alternative workplace during the employee's normal working hours to ensure proper maintenance of Government-owned property and conformance with safety standards. (Agencies may require employees to complete a self-certification safety checklist.)

Alternative Workplace Costs

The employee understands that the Government will not be responsible for any operating costs that are associated with the employee using his or her home as an alternative worksite, for example, home maintenance, insurance, or utilities. The employee understands he or she does not relinquish any entitlement to reimbursement for authorized expenses incurred while conducting business for Government, as provided for by statute and regulations.

Injury Compensation

Employee understands he or she is covered under the Federal Employee's Compensation Act if injured in the course of actually performing official duties at the regular office or the alternative duty station. The employee agrees to notify the supervisor immediately of any accident or injury that occurs at the alternative workplace and to complete any required forms. The supervisor agrees to investigate such a report immediately.

Work Assignments/Performance

Employee agrees to complete all assigned work according to procedures mutually agreed upon by the employee and the supervisor and according to guidelines and standards in the employee performance plan. The employee agrees to provide regular reports if required by the supervisor to help judge performance. The employee understands that a decline in performance may be grounds for cancelling the alternative workplace agreement.

Disclosure

Employee agrees to protect Government/agency records from unauthorized disclosure or damage and will comply with requirements of the Privacy Act of 1974, 5 USC 552a.

Standards of Condct

Employee agrees he or she is bound by agency standards of conduct while working at the alternative worksite.

Cancellation

Agency agrees to let employees resume his or her regular schedule at the regular office after notice to the supervisor. Employee understands that the agency may cancel the telecommuting arrangement and instruct the employee to resume working at the regular office. The agency agrees to follow any applicable administrative or negotiated procedures.

Other Action

Nothing in this agreement precludes the agency from taking any appropriate disciplinary or adverse action against an employee who fails to comply with the provisions of this agreement.

Employee's Signature and Date   _____

Supervisor's Signature and Date   _____

2

Employer/ employee telework agreement

Here is an example of an employer/employee telework agreement as used by Pacific Bell in California

TELECOMMUTING AGREEMENT
I have read and understand the attached Management Telecommuting and Virtual Office Policy, and agree to the duties, obligations, responsibilities and conditions for telecommuters expressed in that document, in addition to my normal duties, obligations and responsibilities as a Pacific Bell management employee.

As a telecommuter, I have reviewed the three kinds of telecommuting on the Telecommuting and Virtual Office Decision Tree Matrix with my supervisor and understand that the kind of telecommuting that applies to my situation is the following:

(specify kind of telecommuting that is being undertaken with amount of frequency)

I agree that, among other things, I am responsible for establishing specific scheduled telecommuting work hours, furnishing and maintaining my designated work space in a safe manner, employing appropriate telecommuting security measures and protecting company assets, information, trade secrets, and information systems. If I have a homebased office, I am responsible for ergonomic requirements for my home-based office.

I understand that telecommuting is voluntary and I may stop telecommuting at will, at any time. I also understand that the company may, at will, at any time, change any or all of the conditions under which I am permitted to telecommute or withdraw permission to telecommute.

Employer/employee telework agreement

Additionally, I have completed the following pertinent sections.

1. Remote Work Location:

    _____
    Street Address

    _____ _____ _____
    City   State   Zip Code

    ☐ Employee Residence ☐ Company Premise ☐ Other

    Description of Designated Work Space at remote work location:

    _____

2. Telecommuting Schedule:
    ☐ On a weekly basis as follows: _____
       (regular telecommuting days)
    ☐ On a monthly basis as follows: _____
       (regular telecommuting dates)
    ☐ No regular schedule – separate permission for each telecommuting day

3. Regular Telecommuting Work Hours: _____ to _____

4. Company Assets (if any) provided for use at remote work location:

    Description   ID Number

    _____ _____

    _____ _____

5. Company Information Systems (if any) to which employee will have access from remote work location:

    _____

    _____

6. Non-Company equipment, software and data permitted to be used with Company Assets or Company Information Systems (if any) to which employee has access from remote work location:

    Item   Company Assets/Information Systems
                                   with which item can be used

    _____ _____

    _____ _____

7. Other:

_____   _____
Dated   Employee Signature

_____   _____
Dated   Supervisor Signature

3 Daily time-sheets

Then consider the use of a daily time-sheet to keep track of work performed and how long it took.

STATE OF CALIFORNIA – DEPARTMENT OF TRANS-PORTATION

TELECOMMUTING DAILY LOG

NAME		BRANCH	UNIT

DATE	TIME	TOTAL HOURS	WORK PERFORMED

STATE OF CALIFORNIA – DEPARTMENT OF TRANSPORTATION

TELECOMMUTING SCHEDULE FOR SUPERVISORS

	FULL DAYS TELECOMMUTING	**PARTIAL DAYS TELECOMMUTING**

TELECOMMUTER	Week(s) of: _____
HOME PHONE NUMBER	M☐ T☐ W☐ TH☐ F☐ M☐ T☐ W☐ TH☐ F☐

TELECOMMUTER	Week(s) of: _____
HOME PHONE NUMBER	M☐ T☐ W☐ TH☐ F☐ M☐ T☐ W☐ TH☐ F☐

TELECOMMUTER	Week(s) of: _____
HOME PHONE NUMBER	M☐ T☐ W☐ TH☐ F☐ M☐ T☐ W☐ TH☐ F☐

TELECOMMUTER	Week(s) of: _____
HOME PHONE NUMBER	M☐ T☐ W☐ TH☐ F☐ M☐ T☐ W☐ TH☐ F☐

TELECOMMUTER	Week(s) of: _____
HOME PHONE NUMBER	M☐ T☐ W☐ TH☐ F☐ M☐ T☐ W☐ TH☐ F☐

TELECOMMUTER	Week(s) of: _____
HOME PHONE NUMBER	M☐ T☐ W☐ TH☐ F☐ M☐ T☐ W☐ TH☐ F☐

4 Safety checklist

To make sure that work safety meets legal requirements this checklist agreement works very well indeed.

United States Office of Personal Management
Sample Self-certification Safety Checklist for Home-based Telecommuters

The following checklist is designed to assess the overall safety of your alternate duty station. Please read and complete the self-certification safety checklist.

Upon completion, you and your supervisor should sign and date the checklist in the spaces provided.

Name:_____ Organization:_____

Address: _____ City/State: _____

Business Telephone: _____ Telecommuting Coordinator: _____

The alternate duty station is _____

Describe the designated work area in the alternate duty station.

_____

A. Workplace Environment

1. Are temperature, noise ventilation and lighting levels adequate for maintaining your normal level of job performance?   Yes [ ] No [ ]

2. Are all stairs with four or more steps equipped with handrails?   Yes [ ] No [ ]

3. Are all circuit breakers and/or fuses in the electrical panel labelled as to intended service?   Yes [ ] No [ ]

4. Do circuit breakers clearly indicate if they are in the open or closed position?   Yes [ ] No [ ]

5. Is all electrical equipment free of recognized hazards that would cause physical harm (frayed wires, bare conductors, loose wires, flexible wires running through walls, exposed wires to the ceiling)   Yes [ ] No [ ]

6. Will the building's electrical system permit the grounding of electrical equipment?   Yes [ ] No [ ]

7. Are aisles, doorways, and corners free of obstruction to permit visibility and movement?   Yes [ ] No [ ]

8. Are file cabinets and storage closets arranged so drawers and doors do not open into walkways?   Yes [ ] No [ ]

9. Do chairs have any loose casters (wheels) and are the rungs and legs of the chairs sturdy?   Yes [ ] No [ ]

10. Are the phone lines, electrical cords, and extension wires secured under a desk or alongside a baseboard?   Yes [ ] No [ ]

11. Is the office space neat, clean, and free of excessive amounts of combustibles?   Yes [ ] No [ ]

12. Are floor surfaces clean, dry, level, and free of worn or frayed seams?   Yes [ ] No [ ]

13. Are carpets well secured to the floor and free of frayed or worn seams?   Yes [ ] No [ ]

14. Is there enough light for reading?   Yes [ ] No [ ]

B. Computer Workstation (if applicable)

15. Is your chair adjustable?	Yes [ ] No [ ]
16. Do you know how to adjust your chair?	Yes [ ] No [ ]
17. Is your back adequately supported by a backrest?	Yes [ ] No [ ]
18. Are your feet on the floor or fully supported by a footrest?	Yes [ ] No [ ]
19. Are you satisfied with the placement of your monitor and keyboard?	Yes [ ] No [ ]
20. Is it easy to read the text on your screen?	Yes [ ] No [ ]
21. Do you need a document holder?	Yes [ ] No [ ]
22. Do you have enough leg room at your desk?	Yes [ ] No [ ]
23. Is the screen free from noticeable glare?	Yes [ ] No [ ]
24. Is the top of the screen eye level?	Yes [ ] No [ ]
25. Is there space to rest the arms while not keying?	Yes [ ] No [ ]
26. When keying, are your forearms close to parallel with the floor?	Yes [ ] No [ ]
27. Are your wrists fairly straight when keying?	Yes [ ] No [ ]

_____   _____
Employee's Signature   Date

_____   _____
Immediate Supervisor's Signature   Date

Approved [ ]   Disapproved [ ]

Please return a copy of this form to your flexiplace coordinator.

Supplies checklist

This might not be exhaustive, but it will get you started. Plus: think about those special needs for your business.

SUPPLIES CHECKLIST FOR THE OFF-SITE OFFICE

_____ Business cards

_____ Calculator

_____ Calendar

_____ Computer supplies

     – Computer disks

     – Printer paper and ribbons

_____ Envelopes

_____ Erasers

_____ Files (folders and labels)

_____ Organization chart

_____ Paper

_____ Paper clips

_____ Rubber bands

_____ Ruler

_____ Scissors

_____ Stacking organization trays

     – In box

     – Out box

_____ Staple remover

_____ Stapler, staples

_____ Tape, transparent

_____ Telephone directory

_____ Writing instruments

     (pens, pencils and sharpener, markers)

Case study – Proto-Type

PROTO-TYPE, Essex CN17 8BG, UK, telephone +44 (0) 1376 561010, fax/modem +44 (0) 1376 562899: a specialized home-based secretarial service is entirely based on telework. Instead of creating your own teleworkers you can use these type of services as an alternative.

OUTLINE OF SERVICE PROVISION

1 Proto-Type provides a home-based secretarial service to clients using fax/modem communication via the existing telephone lines.
2 The home-based secretaries (teleworkers) provide their own computer, word processing software, printer, telephone line and are responsible for the provision and payment of all consumables such as stationary, telephone expenses etc. In addition, if they do not already have an existing fax/modem, then we provide such equipment on a hire basis.
3 The teleworkers are registered with us and we, in turn, register them with our clients, according to their background, experience and word processing.
4 Proto-Type interview all teleworkers before they register to ensure that they have the experience appropriate to our clients. Also that their computer hardware and software is suitable for using modern communication and is compatible with that of the client.
5 Our clients use the service by contacting the teleworkers direct. Manuscript documents are faxed by the client to the teleworker, typed and returned to the client via the modem.
6 The teleworkers record the hours spent working for a particular client and invoice Proto-Type at an agreed contract rate per hour. Proto-Type would in turn invoice the client in accordance with their agreed terms.

7   A Proto-Type representative would periodically visit the teleworkers to carry out quality checks and to resolve any difficulties they might be experiencing. In addition, Proto-Type administer their payments and continue to market the service so as to provide continuity of work. Proto-Type also carry out client liaison to ensure that they are completely satisfied with the service.

8   Proto-Type have secured the services of a number of qualified bi- and trilingual secretaries and are able to offer a translation service in French, Italian, German and Spanish at considerably reduced rates to those charged by translation agencies.

9   Proto-Type also undertake the transcription of audio tapes. These are sent via mail to the teleworkers who type the documents and again return them to the client via the modem. However, we are currently exploring a number of solutions to enable the transfer of audio transcription via the telephone.

24 January 1996

PROTO-TYPE: The Concept

It is a primary objective of any business to keep overheads to a minimum while maintaining human resources at an optimum level. Never more so than in the current economic climate. Running a secretarial resource at the optimum level is particularly difficult with the fluctuating demands from all levels of management. Agency staff are generally the answer, but again a delicate balance has to be achieved. In addition, the quality of agency staff can vary and the learning process of your particular word processing software and general office systems can create inefficiencies leading to management frustrations.

Proto-Type provides an innovative solution to resourcing your typing requirements. We operate a remote network of highly skilled and qualified secretaries/personal assistants. Communication with this network is via telephone, fax and modem and our operating hours are totally flexible.

Being non-office based our network personnel do not have direct or indirect commuting costs nor do they need to demand the inner-city salary levels that you are currently paying your permanent staff. As a result we can offer a service that will meet your demands quickly and at a rate that is considerably cheaper than any other facility that you are currently using.

Proto-Type staff have been personally selected for their speed, accuracy and overall experience. The majority have been personal assistants/secretaries to company directors and therefore respect the confidential nature of their work. All personnel are interviewed and are required to sign a 'Declaration of Confidentiality'. In addition, we will provide the curricula vitae of the secretaries we feel are best suited to your business activity.

Proto-Type may either be used simply to meet your peak periods or you may wish to use our facility as a permanent feature of your office structure.

Proto-Type invoice on a time charge basis. The hours worked by each secretary are accurately recorded and closely monitored by our management. This means that unlike your permanent or agency staff you only pay for productive time. Quality checks are made continuously to ensure that our secretaries maintain the highest standards.

We summarize below the benefits of using Proto-Type:

- Clients can maintain an optimum level of permanent secretarial assistance.
- Typing can be resourced to meet any time requirement, night and weekend working.
- In-house secretaries are relieved of copy typing so that they concentrate on more cost effective tasks.
- We can provide a resource when in-house secretaries are absent or when work load is at a peak.
- There is no need to employ agency staff at premium rates.
- You only pay for productive time.

PROTO-TYPE: The System

Each of our home-based secretaries is equipped with a personal computer, word processing software, a fax/modem and a printer. We will ensure that the word processing software used by the registered secretary is compatible with that of the client.

The client will be required to provide us with their standard letter or report layout specifying the margins, justification and font.

At the beginning of each week Proto-Type will provide the client with a register which will provide the name, telephone/fax/modem number and daily availability of each secretary. The register will contain any number of secretaries according to the client's requirements.

Manuscript documents may be faxed to any one of the secretaries on the register and the typed document will be returned to the client via a modem-to-modem connection.

The client will be required to install their own modem and communication software to a PC which will require a dedicated telephone line. Communication with the in-house secretaries via a local area network is an ideal arrangement. We would be happy to advise on these installations, and in particular to ensure that appropriate network security systems are set up.

Documents that are returned to the client are retrieved by the in-house secretary, printed and returned to the author for approval in the normal way. Any corrections to the document can be made locally and the final version printed out.

Charges:

Pricing structure for London clients is on a time-charge basis which is £10.00 per hour or part thereof for work undertaken during normal working hours. There is a percentage increase for evening and weekend working. We also provide a language translation service which, again for London-based clients, is £18.00 per hour (with the percentage increase as above).

These rates compare favourably with secretarial agencies and particularly translation agencies.

7 Finnish Ministry of Labour telework questionnaire

This questionnaire has two immediate uses. First, it can help you think about your telework needs and requirements. Second, it can be a useful assessment for older managers and supervisors on how teleworking meets the needs of people and the business.

D1   The use of telework and experience of it:

Please assess to what extent your enterprise employs teleworkers

		Not at all	A few	Some	A considerable number	Very many	Don't know
1	Occasionally, within working hours	1	2	3	4	5	9
2	Occasionally, as overtime	1	2	3	4	5	9
3	Regularly	1	2	3	4	5	9
4	Regularly, full-time	1	2	3	4	5	9

If you answer 'not at all' or 'don't know' move on to D2.

Which of the following modes of teleworking are used in your enterprise?

		Yes	No	Don't know	Comments
5	Teleworking both at home and at the office, no special arrangements	____	_____	_____	_____
6	Teleworking both at home and at the office, as part of an experiment or a project	____	_____	_____	_____
7	Teleworking solely at home	____	_____	_____	_____

8 Mobile teleworking   ____ _____ _____   _____
9 Commissioned work   ____ _____ _____   _____
   (freelancing and other
   self-employment)
10 In a satellite office of   ____ _____ _____   _____
   your own organization
11 Other, list:

_____
_____

12 Which jobs in your enterprise are carried out by telework?

_____
_____

What were in your opinion the reasons that led to the introduction of telework in your enterprise?

	Yes	No	Don't know	Comments
13 Recruiting skilled staff	___	___	___	___
14 Motivation of personnel	___	___	___	___
15 Retaining key personnel	___	___	___	___
16 Distributing the work load	___	___	___	___
17 More effective use of time	___	___	___	___
18 Overtime work	___	___	___	___
19 Cost of office space	___	___	___	___
20 Productivity or efficiency of work	___	___	___	___
21 Other, list:	___	___	___	___

22 What in your opinion, are the advantages of teleworking?

_____
_____
_____
_____

23 What in your opinion, are the disadvantages of teleworking?

_____
_____
_____
_____

2 Interest in using telework or extending it:

To what extent might your company by interested in introducing telework or extending its use with regard to the following modes of teleworking?

	Not at all interested	Not very interested	Somewhat interested	Very interested	Extremely interested	Don't know
1 Employees who spend all their working hours at home	1	2	3	4	5	9
2 Employees who spend only part of their working time at home	1	2	3	4	5	9
3 Employees who work in local telework centres (neighbourhood work centres)	1	2	3	4	5	9
4 Teleworkers who work for your enterprise in a satellite office	1	2	3	4	5	9
5 Teleworkers whose work involves travelling (mobile telework)	1	2	3	4	5	9
6 Telework under contract to your enterprise (self-employed)	1	2	3	4	5	9

To what extent in your opinion do the following factors limit the introduction of telework in your enterprise?

	Not at all	Very little	To some extent	To a considerable extent	Very much	Don't know
7 Lack of training or insufficient knowledge of how to organize telework	1	2	3	4	5	9
8 The high cost of computer hardware and telecom services	1	2	3	4	5	9

	Not at all	Very little	To some extent	To a considerable extent	Very much	Don't know
9 Causes related to the productivity or quality of work	1	2	3	4	5	9
10 Difficulties in monitoring and management	1	2	3	4	5	9
11 Problems relating to organizing communications	1	2	3	4	5	9
12 Insufficiency of social contacts	1	2	3	4	5	9
13 Opposition from trade unions	1	2	3	4	5	9
14 Other reasons, list:						

Background information
1 Principal line of business
2 Number of personnel

_____	2–4	_____	50–99
_____	5–9	_____	100–499
_____	10–19	_____	500 or more
_____	20–49		

3 Turnover approximately _____
4 Structure of operations (number of different locations)

Further action:

May we contact you or your representative later with regard to
1 Organizing telework? _____ Yes _____ No
2 Organization of business cooperation _____ Yes _____ No

Contact data: name and position in enterprise, tel. no.

_____

Address to which feedback can be sent

_____

Thank you for your assistance

8

Teleworking at Pacific Bell

Pacific Bell is a leader in Telework. Their experiences and observations are worthy of more than a second look. Use them as a guide to your own plans and benchmark your experiences against these.

Pacific Bell

Remote management is not much different from managing people on-site. It involves basic management skills which include setting goals, assessing progress, giving regular feedback, and managing by results. In fact, managers of telecommuters have reported that their own overall management skills increased.

Management by Objectives

You have probably managed by objectives in one form or another by:

- Setting goals or objectives
- Action-planning to work on objectives
- Corrective actions
- Periodic reviews and performance appraisals

When setting objectives and giving performance feedback, remember the following:

- Employee participation promotes acceptance of the manager's observations.
- Performance objectives should be clear and specific.
- Productivity improvement is more likely if problem areas are discussed right away.
- Criticism triggers defensive reactions. Talk about how something can be improved, rather than spending too much time on the downside of an employee's work.

Teleworking

Measuring performance

Have clearly defined objectives and measurable output. Performance evaluation should not be different for on-site and off-site workers. If you feel current measurement criteria are not sufficient, this will be an opportunity to redevelop them. Be careful not to over-measure, not every task can be evaluated in quantitative terms. Evaluate individual work as well as group work. Telecommuters often sustain or even increase individual productivity levels, but their group work may suffer because they are not staying in touch with co-workers.

Management resistance

Some managers feel a loss of control when their employees are not in close contact. Others feel that managing telecommuters is a burden. It can become a burden if too many people in your department are telecommuting and schedules need to be juggled, or if the telecommuter's co-workers come to you with questions that the telecommuter should be answering. Training and communication mechanisms can be initiated to avoid these problems. If the telecommuters' schedules are getting out of hand, assign a day or two each week for face-to-face meetings. If co-workers are having difficulty getting their jobs done because the telecommuter is not accessible, find out why. As long as you are able to resolve communications and scheduling issues and can measure output, you should find you telecommuters no less productive than the in-office workers.

Multiple telecommuters in a department

If there are jobs in your department suitable for telecommuting, more than one employee is likely to be eligible for the program. Be aware of how many telecommuters you can manage at any given time. Before you approve too many telecommuting arrangements, you might want to gain experience with a smaller number of them. If an additional telecommuter will create a burden on the department, explain to the group that it is not feasible. When necessary, telecommuters may return to on-site work. A rotating schedule or fewer individual telecommuting hours might be the solution.

Employees not suitable for telecommuting

Employees not familiar with telecommuting tend to think of it as a way to escape the office. Contrary to popular belief, telecommuting involves hard work, dedication and adjustment.

Telecommuters will be isolated from co-workers. They no longer have an office mate with whom to interact. They have to discipline themselves to get started and stay on track. If an employee is unsuitable, discuss any characteristics the employee could change (organization skills, self discipline). Re-evaluate the option in six months. If an employee is not performing at an adequate level in all aspects of the job, telecommuting should not be an option. A telecommuter whose productivity drops below acceptable levels should work on-site until his or her performance has improved.

The manager's role

Schedule regular meetings with the telecommuter to assess needs, giving feedback, and discuss problems. These meetings will enable you to maintain contact and the telecommuter will be less isolated. Regular meetings for setting timetables and assessing progress will give employees deadlines to keep them on target. When face-to-face meetings are not possible, utilize other means to keep the lines of communication open. You may want to assign a key contact person (see 'Key contact' below) to keep your telecommuters aware of happenings around the office.

Co-workers

Once an employee has a start date for telecommuting, inform others in the work group what times that employee will be out of the office and how they can be reached in the remote work space. Co-workers should be notified when telecommuters will be working outside standard work hours.

Office workers and telecommuters should plan for whatever face-to-face meetings may be necessary. Telecommuters should be highly accessible. Their voice mail messages should indicate that they are out of the office, and provide a means by which they can be contacted.

Key contact

Telecommuting should not put an extra strain on the workers in the office. Communication is the best solution to this potential problem. Always inform co-workers of schedules and projects that concern them. A key contact person in the office can keep both telecommuters and office workers aware of important events. The contact can also assist with favours such as getting information from a file or sending a fax, as long as these favours are not being requested too frequently.

Administrative support

The administrator supporting the telecommuter should know all the details of the agreement. When people call or come by looking for the telecommuter, the administrator can explain that the employee is working off-site, and give them the number where he or she can be reached.

Clients

Clients are people both inside and outside your company. Extend them the same courtesy you would co-workers. Telecommuters should let clients know they are working from home, and inform them of the schedule. It's good to remind them fairly frequently: 'Call Mondays, Wednesdays or Fridays in the office; Tuesdays and Thursdays at home.'

Tips for managing telecommuters
- Trust your telecommuters
- Get to know them
- Encourage team relationships

Manage by measuring results
- Set goals and objectives with telecommuters
- Provide routine and timely feedback
- Set deadlines
- Delegate assignments equitably between teelcommuters and non-telecommuters
- Recognize results

Communicate
- Include telecommuters in appropriate communications and meetings
- Use various forms of communication with all employees (e-mail, phone, face-to-face meetings, etc.)
- Encourage interaction with all team members
- Reinforce timely two-way communication

Teleworking at Pacific Bell

Support telecommuting

- Take telecommuting seriously
- Require participation in surveys and the evaluation process
- Use a telecommuting agreement
- Provide appropriate training
- Be prepared to expand the telecommuting program or allow employees to withdraw from the program
- Celebrate the success

9

US Department of Transportation telecommuting guidelines

Next, use these US Department of Transportation guidelines to overcome problems and areas of misunderstanding and contention

GAINING AGREEMENT: HOW CAN YOU WORK WITH YOUR MANAGER TO ENSURE SUCCESS?

The Importance of Joint Planning and Work Agreements

Telecommuting arrangements should include a written agreement between the manager and the telecommuter that outlines the organizational policies and logistics of the telecommuting arrangement. A sample work agreement for government employees is provided in the Telecommuting Manual.

This agreement includes such issues as: the time period for participating in the program, the official and alternate duty stations, hours of duty and timekeeping procedures, work assignment and reporting requirements, and other policy and procedure criteria.

In addition to a general work agreement, telemanagers and telecommuters should jointly establish performance goals and objectives (or progress-reporting procedures and associated expectations), with timetables and deadlines clearly spelled out, as well as additional work procedure details appropriate for their particular office setting. The level of detail in these procedures and expectations depends on factors such as the manager's style of supervision, the telecommuter's communication style, job requirements, and organizational needs.

TELECOMMUTER PLANNING AND DISCUSSION GUIDE (for use in joint planning with the manager)

The following discussion guide and checklist will help you as you plan your telecommuting arrangement with your manager. Although the questions are written for you to ask your manager, they are intended as a guide only. The main purpose of this guide is to open a dialogue between you and your manager in which both individual's perspectives are discussed, key telecommuting issues are covered, and decisions are made before telecommuting begins. As you complete discussion of each question with your manager, check off the question; when you have completed all the questions and/or before you attend the discussion session, you and your manager should sign and date in the space provided at the end of the list. Bring the signed list to the discussion session, return it to your coordinator, or follow other instructions as provided by your coordinator.

Preliminary

Have we both signed a general telecommuting agreement?
What organizational policies and procedures exist about telecommuting?
Have the telecommuting selection criteria been shared with all staff members?
If applicable, have we visited the telecenter and selected a suitable workstation?
Have we determined my hardware, software, and telecommunications needs?
Have we ensured that the alternate worksite is adequately equipped?

Procedures

How many days should I telecommute? Should we ease into this agreement, beginning with one day per week and increasing later?
How will I receive messages from callers or visitors I have missed?
How will I communicate my schedule and contact information with other staff members? with customers?

Teleworking

How will we handle last-minute meetings and/or crises that arise on telecommuting days?

Which of my duties do you think are telecommutable? Which ones would you prefer I work on in the office?

Employee–manager Relationship

What concerns, if any, do you have about my participation as a telecommuter?

What goals and objectives should we establish for the telecommuting arrangement?

What interim and final due dates should we set for assigned tasks?

How will I get in formation about projects, educational or advancement opportunities, office events, etc.?

How often should I check in, if at all, on telecommuting days? With whom?

Co-worker Communications

How will we respond to co-worker sensitivities and concerns about my telecommuting?

How will you discuss with my co-workers the selection criteria and my selection?

Taking Care of Business: Customer Considerations

To best serve our clients, how do we want to inform internal or external customers of the telecommuting arrangement, if at all?

Are procedures in place that will prevent or minimize any inconvenience or additional expense to customers?

Assessing the Arrangement

How and how often should we assess how well the telecommuting arrangement is working and make adjustments, as needed?

_____   _____

(Telecommuter signature)   (Manager signature)

Date _____

150

10 US Department of Transportation - Orientation to Telecommuting

In setting a style for yourself and others to effectively, fairly and productively manage teleworkers use this US Department of Transportation – Orientation to Telecommuting. Think about and answer the following questions honestly to yourself:

1 Are you or are you willing to focus on facilitating the accomplishment of work by managing the flow of work as opposed to the worker? Can you act as a facilitator and not as a 'boss' or 'supervisor'? Do you need to feel that you are 'the boss', that you are 'in charge', that you control what people do, or that you have power over people?

2 Do you feel a certain status in being the boss and that you would lose that status with facilitative management?

3 Do you think that your subordinates would not respect you as a facilitative manager?

4 Are you willing to delegate responsibility for work to the person who is assigned to do it? Do you believe that you have to monitor and control the work or it won't be done? Do you believe that your value, usefulness, status, etc. would be jeopardized by pushing responsibility to the level of the worker? For example, if there is a request from top management for an oral report on a specific task accomplished by one of your subordinates, do you feel that you, not the person who actually performed the work, should make the report?

5 Are you willing to allow workers to do the work in their own ways as long as they complete the work in an acceptable (quantity, quality, timeliness) fashion? Do you need to see the worker or can you evaluate job performance on the basis of work output? Some telecommuters report that they miss out on promotions and choice assignments, that these are given to those who provide 'face time' to the manager; does that apply to you?

6 Do you believe the organization and its management should focus on the bottom line and not on workers' quality of life? Do you believe that work is more important than the people who perform it? Are the personal needs of your organization's employees important to you? Do you believe that you should do everything in your power to assist your employee's balance their work and personal life requirements?

7 Do you like, personally, the role of facilitative manager? Do you like people? Some managers feel coerced into different roles or into accepting telecommuting programs; how do you feel? Some managers who feel coerced end up taking it out on the telecommuters by creating unnecessary hurdles and discomforts, excessive controls, rigid procedures, or by otherwise sabotaging the program; do you feel such an inclination? The same questions apply to managers who are nervous or fearful of the program.

There is no set profile of answer to these questions. They are guidelines to reviewing your role as a manager. If you are truly honest, you won't have all 'yes' or all 'no' answers. Think about your answers and use your thoughts to determine:

■ If you're ready to manage a telecommuter
■ What adjustments you should make to make the program mutually satisfying to you and the telecommuter.

MANAGERIAL STYLE, EXPECTATION, AND TELECOMMUTING

Managers do not always consider the effect of managerial and communication style on the telecommuting arrangement. Some managers require more interaction with staff members, while others prefer to let employees pursue their work with little direct supervisory input. Either of these styles can work in telecommuting situation, if telecommuting plans and procedures are established that respond to these styles issues. While there is no 'one best style' of management for telecommuting, it is important to include style considerations as you plan or telecommuting. Your sensitivity to and patience with everyone's adjustment (including yours!) to a new telecommuting arrangement will contribute to its success.

Use the following to assess your own style and expectations. Answer the questions below about your office situation. Think about your answers and determine what, if any, actions you should take or discussions you should have to ensure that your style and expectations match your telecommuting program planning and preparation.

1 In general how much autonomy do your staff members have – whether they are telecommuting or not?
2 How important to you are changes that may occur in the telecommuter's morale and interactions with co-workers?
3 What is your likely reaction if changes occur in other staff members' job performance, morale and coordination with the telecommuter? Do you expect others will want to participate? Is that a concern?
4 What effect will telecommuting have on the telecommuter's assigned projects and/or chances for advancement?
5 To what extent do you currently set specific performance objectives for staff members? How will this change with telecommuters?
6 What criteria do you use to evaluate staff performance for positions similar to the telecommuting position(s)?
7 Considering the nature of your staff member's work, what is the maximum amount of time you would want him or her to telecommute?
8 What changes do you expect you will have to make to manage your telecommuter effectively?

US Department of Health policy procedures

This is how the US Department of Health outlines its policy procedures and its wants and needs analysis. It is easily adaptable to other businesses and industries.

POLICY PROCEDURE – SAMPLE

Purpose/Introduction

To encourage and set the standards for a consistent process and treatment of employees regarding requests for telecommuting and to ensure success in the alternative work arrangement. The Department of Health (DOH) recognizes the potential of telecommuting as a viable worksite alternative that, when appropriately applied, benefits both the agency and the individual employee.

Telecommuting is a voluntary workplace alternative available through a mutually agreed upon arrangement between an employee and his/her supervisor. The arrangement is not permanent and may be terminated by the employee or supervisor at any time as agreed upon in the Telecommuting Authorization.

Telecommuting is the use of telecommunications and computer technologies to allow some employees to regularly perform some of their assigned duties at other than the conventional workplace during assigned work hours, up to a specified number of days a week. The alternate workplace could be the home, a satellite office closer to the employee's home, or a neighbourhood work center that provides workspace and equipment for telecommuters from a variety of organizations.

Policies

1. Eligibility

All DOH permanent employees not in a trial service or in-training status are eligible to apply for telecommuting. Approval shall be based on the requesting employee meeting all of the following criteria:

- The nature of the work requires minimal face-to-face inter-action, or can be scheduled to permit telecommuting;
- There is minimal need for specialized material or equipment or it is at least capable of being scheduled to permit telecommuting;
- The employee's job is not dependent upon location of the workplace, and has tasks and deliverables that can be clearly defined and monitored at other than the traditional **worksite**;
- The employee's absence from the office is not detrimental to the productivity of the work group.

2. Performance characteristics

Performance characteristics of potential telecommuters include ability to perform his/her work requirements, job knowledge, competence, and reliability as shown by the employee meeting 'normal requirements' in all areas of his/her most recent Employee Performance Evaluation.

Other criteria include:

- Employee's and supervisor's willingness to sign and abide by the terms of the Telecommuting Authorization and these policies.
- Support and willingness of the supervisor to invest the necessary time to help the telecommuting arrangement succeed.
- Willingness of both the employee and supervisor to participate fully in any required telecommuting training and evaluation efforts.
- The supervisor's demonstrated ability to establish clear objectives, measure performance by results and maintain a flexible management approach.
- Telecommuting will not change salary, responsibilities or benefits.

■ The telecommuter's salary, responsibilities, **work time** and state-provided benefits will not **change as a result of** telecommuting.

3. Professional Standards To Be Maintained
Job standards will be maintained while telecommuting.

4. Telecommuting Authorization Signed by Employee and Supervisor
A Telecommuting Authorization based on the needs of DOH, the job, and the work group will be signed by the employee and supervisor describing the mutually agreed upon arrangement. The Authorization will provide a specific understanding of the arrangement and the joint responsibilities for each.

5. MSR (WAC), FLSA, OFM, and DOH Travel Policies Apply
Existing Merit System Rules (WAC) on leave, hours of work and scheduling work: Fair Labour Standards Act (FLSA) rules on overtime; Office of Financial Management (OFM) and DOH travel policies and regulations shall apply to telecommuters. When telecommuting, the alternate worksite is the official station for travel expense voucher purposes except that travel to and from the employee's regular DOH office shall not be a reimbursable expense. For employees in a 'scheduled' work period designation, supervisors and telecommuting employees must ensure compliance with FLSA and WAC rules on overtime. Telecommuting shall not be authorized unless compliance is assured.

6. Performance Evaluation Requirements
Performance evaluation requirements shall not change, although the supervisor's method of monitoring and evaluating performance will likely focus on results and process rather than direct observation. Deadlines, goals and objectives must be clearly communicated.

7. Employees Must Comply with DOH Rules, Policies, Practices
Employees shall comply with all DOH rules, policies, practices and instructions. Failure to do so may result in removal from the telecommunting program and/or disciplinary action.

8. Employees in Union Bargaining Unit May Telecommute Unless Prohibited by Agreement

Employeesd within a bargaining unit may be included in the telecommuting program unless prohibited by the collective bargaining agreement.

9. Assisting Disabled Worker/Return to Work

Supervisors and employees may consider telecommuting as a flexible workplace arrangement for assisting disabled workers, or in returning to work those employees injured on the job and on worker's compensation. Also, please refer to DOH Policy/ Procedure 07.022 regarding reasonable accommodation.

10. Cost–benefit Are Consideration

Each telecommuting arrangement must be reviewed for cost–benefit (tangibles and intangibles). The nature of the job requirements and expected results are considerations for individual determinations.

11. Costs Are Responsibility of Employee's Work Unit

Costs associated with telecommuting are the responsibility of and will be charged to employee's work unit.

12. Telecommuters Must Have Adequate Time in Office

The amount of time spent telecommuting during a work week may vary according to each job, equipment needs and the individual Telecommuting Authorization. Minimally it must allow adequate in-office time for meetings, access to facilities and supplies and to maintain the telecommuter's involvement and communication with other employees, customers and DOH events.

13. Supervisor or Other Authorized Person Providing Telecommuter's Home Phone Number

Only the employee's supervisor or persons authorized by the employee will be provided a telecommuter's home phone number.

14. Term of Telecommuting is Twelve Months

The maximum term of a telecommuting arrangement is twelve (12) months, subject to extension. Extensions of the term require re-authorization by completing a new Telecommuting Application and Telecommuting Authorization.

Teleworking

To further describe and clarify the above policies, the following conditions and responsibilities are provided:

Work Hours/Accessibility

■ The number of hours worked will not change because of telecommuting. Work hours will be scheduled and any changes must be approved by the supervisor in advance. Also please refer to DOH Policy/Procedure 07.008 regarding work hours, schedules and Fair Labour Standards Act.

■ While telecommuting may facilitate employees' working around family responsibilities, it is not intended to be a substitute for family care. The employee shall not have the primary responsibility for child care, dependent adult or other duties not ordinarily part of his or her job duties during working hours.

■ Telecommuters will maintain accessibility to their supervisor, co-worker and customers as agreed upon in the Telecommuting Authorization.

■ Request to work overtime must receive advance approval and requests for leave shall be reported and/or approved by the supervisor, in a manner consistent with DOH policy.

■ If an office closure or emergency excuses other employees from working and work can proceed at the alternative worksite, telecommuters are not excused from working. However, an employee may be excused from working for an emergency such as a power failure that affects the alternative worksite but not the office, or may be required to report to the regular office. The immediate supervisor is to be notified of the emergency and shall excuse the employee or require attendance at the regular office.

Computer Equipment and Software

■ Telecommuters who have their own equipment necessary for telecommuting are encouraged to use it. Appropriate combinations of DOH- and employee-owned equipment and software may be installed, at the option of DOH.

■ Depending on the nature of the job, availability of funds and Information Services technical support capacity, DOH may provide a workstation, software, modem, surge protector, communications software and related computer equipment. Any hardware or software provided by DOH remains the property of DOH and shall be returned at the end of the telecommuting arrangement. The Equipment/Software Inventory form will be completed for assigned DOH equipment to be used off-site.

- Each work unit will be responsible for obtaining assigning inventory processing, installation or maintaining as required, DOH equipment being used for telecommuting. DOH Information Services (IS) is responsible for installation of computer and data communication lines. This may be accomplished by IS staff, by contracting or other means as determined by IS.
- Products, documents, and other records used and/or developed while telecommuting remain the property of and be available to DOH, and are subject to departmental and divisional policies regarding confidentiality and authorization access.
- DOH-owned software may not be duplicated except as formally authorized.
- Telecommuters using DOH software must adhere to the manufacturer's licensing agreements.
- The employee is responsible for protecting the integrity of copyrighted software, and following policies, procedures, and practices related to them to the same extent applicable in the regular office. The employee must take all precautions necessary to avoid contamination of data (for example, by use of unauthorized software that may contain a computer virus).
- All equipment, furniture, software, supplies, or other material purchased or maintained by DOH are to be used by the telecommuter and only for DOH business.
- Purchase/maintenance of personal office furniture or equipment (e.g. desks, file cabinets, answering devices, etc.) is the telecommuter's responsibility.
- Restricted access documents and other material may not be taken out of the regular DOH office without prior supervisory approval.

Workstation Equipment Maintenance, Repair and Information Services Technical Support

- Employees who elect to use their own equipment (not furnished by DOH) are responsible for its maintenance and repair unless provided for elsewhere in this policy and procedure.

■ The employee has the same responsibility for taking appropriate steps to minimize damage to DOH property at the alternate worksite as would exist at the regular DOH office. DOH assumes no obligation in regard to damage or loss to property owned by the employee at the alternate worksite.

■ Surge protectors will be provided by DOH and must be used with any DOH-owned computer equipment. The employee will be responsible for damage resulting from a power surge if no surge protector is used.

■ DOH Information Services will provide support for the following, with specific agreement with the telecommuter's work unit manager:
  – Installation of DOH hardware and software.
  – Non-DOH-owned equipment on a 'best effort' basis, limited to hardware problems occurring during telecommuting.
  – Support will be provided by extent possible with regard to available DOH Information Services staff, funds, support capacity and other priorities.

Workspace

■ The employee is responsible for establishing and maintaining a designated, adequate workspace at the alternate worksite. The employee is responsible for maintaining this space to the same safety and other standards as are applicable at the regular DOH office.

■ With reasonable notice and at mutually agreed upon times during employees' normal work hours, DOH may make on-site visits for inspection of the workspace to ensure that it is sufficient for the equipment, safe from hazards and/or to install or retrieve DOH equipment or property. Visits may be made by the employee's supervisor, or anyone designated by the supervisor to make an inspection.

Injuries

■ DOH will have the same responsibility for job-related accidents or injuries to the employee at the alternate worksite that it has at the employee's regular DOH office.

■ DOH does not assume responsibility for injury to any persons at the employee's residence or the alternate workspace within it.

160

Communication (Voice-data) Expenses

- Telephone services that are deemed necessary for the employee to do the job will be paid by DOH only if specifically approved by DOH.
- Telecommuters are expected to use the SCAN System when making long-distance, work-related voice communications. Long-distance call charges incurred using other long-distance carriers may be reimbursed as stipulated in the Telecommuting Authorization.

Supplies

Supplies necessary to complete assigned work at the alternate worksite should be obtained during one of the telecommuter's in-office work periods.

Other Costs Are Responsibility of Employee

Individual tax implications, auto/homeowner insurance, and incidental residential utility costs are the responsibility of the employee.

Procedures:

Responsibility	Action
Employee/Telecommuter	- Completes Telecommuting Application and forwards to immediate supervisor. - Signs Telecommuting Authorization form if approved by supervisor
Supervisor	- Approves Telecommuting Application 1 If disapproved, discusses with employee. 2 If approved, prepares and signs Telecommuting Authorization and has employee sign 3 If approved, forwards both forms to Assistant Secretary.
Secretary	- Coordinates with Information Services regarding estimated cost and needs of telecommuter as well as time frame for installation.
Assistant Secretary	- Approves/disapproves Telecommuting Application and Telecommuting Authorization. This includes authorization for costs of telecommuting and processing of orders for hardware and software. 1 If disapproved, returns to supervisor with explanation. 2 If approved, signs both forms, one copy each sent to telecommuter, supervisor, and Information Services. Sends original to Human Resource Office.

Human Resource Office	■ Files Telecommuting Application and Telecommuting Authorization forms in employee's personnel file.
	■ Maintains a listing of telecommuters for statistical purposes
Information Services	■ Assesses data communication needs for the telel-commuter and inform the supervisor of the cost and time frame for installation
	■ Processes orders for hardware and software.

DEPARTMENT OF HEALTH TELECOMMUTING APPLICATION

TELECOMMUTER INFORMATION

1. Name:_____ Job Title: _____

    Division/Section:_____ Work Phone: _____

    Proposed alternate worksite is: ☐ Home _____

    ☐ Other _____

    Alternate worksite Phone: _____ Work Period Designation: _____

PROPOSED TELECOMMUTING DUTIES

2. Describe the types of work you propose to do at the alternate worksite:_____
    _____
    _____

3. Note any special circumstances that should be considered: _____
    _____
    _____

4. Proposed term of telecommuting to begin _____ and end _____
                                           month/day/year   month/day/year

5. I understand that a Telecommuting Authorization must be signed and approved prior to beginning telecommuting.

_____
Employee's signature   Date

_____
Supervisor's signature   Date   ☐ Approved   ☐ Disapproved

_____
Assistant Secretary   Date   ☐ Approved   ☐ Disapproved

Distribution:
Original: Personnel File
Copies: Employee

Supervisor Information Services

6. Telecommuting day will be: _____ Working
    hours on these days will be: _____ to _____
    Core hours of availability and accessibility by phone will be:

    _____

    Employee will be in the DOH office on the following days and times: _____
    Employee agrees to structure his/her time to ensure attendance at required
    meetings as designated by the supervisor.
7. Employee agrees to stay current on DOH events, and facilitate communication
    with customers and co-workers who may be inconvenienced by telecommuting.
8. Employee and supervisor agree on the following work assignments, objectives,
    expected results and criteria to evaluate:

    _____

    _____

9. Hardware and software support per DOH Policy/Procedure is authorized, as follows:

    _____

    _____

10. Additional conditions agreed to by the telecommuter and supervisor.

    _____

    _____

11. This telecommuting arrangement shall being on _____
    and continue until _____ or until ended by the employee or
    employer. Unless otherwise mutually agreed upon, either party shall provide
    minimum notice of _____ days prior to termination of this
    agreement. Violation of the Telecommuting Policy/Procedure, this agreement, or
    initiation of corrective or disciplinary action may cause immediate termination of
    this Telecommuting Authorization.
12. Employee stipulates that he/she will not have primary responsibility for child care,
    dependent care for others, or other non-work related-duties or activities during
    telecommuting working hours.

understand and agree to the terms and conditions of this agreement.

_____   _____
Employee's signature   Date

_____   _____
Supervisor's signature   Date   ☐ Approved   ☐ Disapproved

_____   _____
Assistant Secretary   Date   ☐ Approved   ☐ Disapproved

Distribution:
Original: Personnel File
Copies: Employee
              Supervisor
              Information Services

...in brief   Teleworking

DEPARTMENT OF HEALTH TELECOMMUTING AGREEMENT
EQUIPMENT/SOFTWARE INVENTORY

Complete when DOH-owned equipment is to be used off-site by employees.

Name
_____

Division _____ Section _____

CPU   Tag#, _____ Serial# _____

Description: _____

MONITOR   Tag# _____ Serial# _____
Description: _____

MODEM   Tag# _____ Serial# _____
(if not internal)

Description: _____

PRINTER   Tag# _____ Serial# _____

Description: _____
SOFTWARE
_____
_____
_____

OTHER
_____
_____

I acknowledge receipt of above:

_____ _____
Employee's signature   Date   Supervisor's signature   Date

164

Distribution:
Original: Personnel File
Copies: Employee
            Supervisor
            Information Services

12 AT&T telework guidelines and assessment procedure

AT&T is one of the leaders in telework initiatives. The following material provides guidelines and assessment information vital to any organization's telework planning and execution.

TELECOMMUTING POLICY EXAMPLE

THE POLICY

AT&T supports telecommuting as an alternative work arrangement and encourages supervisors to give employee telecommuting proposals every consideration. Employees may telecommute with prior supervisory approval and as specified in this policy. This policy does not interfere with supervisors allowing employees to occasionally work at home.

Telecommuting can help:

■ Better meet both business and employee needs
■ Attract and retain a diverse and talented workforce
■ Comply with the Clean Air Act and other laws
■ Improve productivity for certain jobs/persons

RESPONSIBILITIES

EMPLOYEES
Telecommuting Employees are responsible to:
- Become familiar with the policy and guidelines for telecommuting, the Telecommuter's Agreement and related documents.
- Propose a telecommuting arrangement to their supervisor.
- Complete and sign the Telecommuter's Agreement and propose required modifications to their supervisors.
- Set up a dedicated home work area that is safe for the employees and others entering it.
- Establish work practices that make the telecommuting arrangement transparent to customers (i.e. ensures customers are not inconvenienced in their dealing with employee or company).
- Abide by the terms and conditions of the Telecommuter's Agreement.
- Report to the work locations, as required, for meetings, training, etc., on request of supervisor or customers.
- Safeguard proprietary information (regardless of form) as specified by company security instructions.
- Determine federal, state and local tax implications resulting from working at home and satisfy their personal tax obligations.
- Comply with applicable state and local zoning ordinances.
- Comply with all other terms and conditions of employment.

SUPERVISORS
Supervisors are responsible to:
- Become familiar with the policy and guidelines for telecommuting, the Telecommuter's Agreement and related documents.
- Consider employee requests to work at home.
- Decide whether a telecommuting arrangement is beneficial to employee and company.
- File original signed Telecommuter's Agreement in the employee personnel files kept by supervisors and retain for one year after telecommuting arrangement ends.
- Give employee a copy of Telecommuter's Agreement.

■ Update Telecommuter's Agreement if any respect of the arrangement covered by the agreement changes.
■ Review company security instructions for computer security and safeguarding proprietary information with employee.
■ Maintain inventory of company-owned equipment in employee's home.
■ Notify appropriate organizations if employee telecommutes from a different state that the work location state.
■ Continue normal supervisory activities including career development, ongoing feedback and performance appraisals.

HUMAN RESOURCES
The Human Resources representative is responsible to:
■ Assist and encourage employees/supervisors wishing to implement telecommuting.
■ Answer questions about telecommuting and help resolve difficulties impeding implementation.

COMPANY
Management is responsible to:
■ Seriously consider telecommuting as a staffing strategy.
■ Encourage telecommuting trials.
■ Recognize supervisors successfully using telecommuting as an alternative work arrangement.

COMPENSATION, BENEFITS, TAXES
Compensation and benefits are not affected by telecommuting.

Telecommuting employees are responsible to determine any federal, state and local tax implications resulting from working at home and to satisfy their personal tax obligations. Employees should refer questions to their personal tax advisor. Tax withholding is impacted when employees telecommute from a different state than their work location site. In these cases, the supervisors need to notify the employee's payroll organization that the employee is telecommuting from a different state than their work state. Provide employee's name, telecommuting schedule, home address and work address.

HOURS OF WORK

An employee's hours of work are unaffected by tele-commuting. The daily schedule is specified in the Telecommuter's Agreement.

The overtime policy extends to telecommuting arrangements. Non-exempt employees must receive compensation for overtime that has been planned, scheduled and authorized in advance by their supervisors. Travel time between an employee's home and regular work location is noncompensable, even if the employee reports to the regular location on a day scheduled for telecommuting.

SAFETY AND ACCIDENTS

Workers' Compensation:

Workers' Compensation liability for illnesses and job-related injuries and eligibility for Accident Disability Benefits continues during the approved work schedule and in the employee's home work area, as described in the Telecommuter's Agreement. Accidents must be reported.

Accidents to Others:

The company is not liable for any injuries to family members, visitors and others in the employee's home. Telecommuting employees should consider carrying insurance that covers third-party injuries arising out of or relating to the use of the home under a telecommuting policy, and should consult their personal insurance carriers for advice.

DISABILITIES

Supervisors may not ask employees on disability to work at home. However, if an employee on disability asks to work at home, the supervisor should consult with and follow the medical professional's advice.

COMPUTER EQUIPMENT AND SECURITY

Telecommuters may use either company-provided or their own computer equipment to perform their jobs from home. In either case, they must abide by company policies covering computer security.

Supervisors should review computer security instructions before the start of a telecommuting arrangement. They must also ensure the Telecommuter's Agreement outlines:

■ The information protection safeguards the employee will implement to protect the equipment and any information stored in it or kept at home.

■ The virus software package the employee will use (any package that is compatible with the computer's operating system is acceptable) to check software for a virus before installing it on equipment used in the home.

COMPANY-PROVIDED EQUIPMENT

An employee's supervisor is responsible for determining whether to authorize company-provided computer equipment for use in an employee's home. If company-provided equipment is used:

■ All maintenance will be performed by an authorized person at a company location at company expense (employee must bring the equipment to the location).

■ The company will repair or replace lost, damaged or stolen equipment provided the employee has taken appropriate precautions to safeguard equipment.

■ Employees may not use company-provided equipment for personal use or allow non-company employees to use it.

■ Employees must return equipment to the company when requested by supervisors or when employment is terminated.

EMPLOYEE-OWNED EQUIPMENT

If employee-owned equipment is used:

■ Expenses (e.g., maintenance, repair, insurance) are employee's responsibility. Company and personal files must be kept on separate removable computing media, clearly marked as company or personal.

■ Software which is not owned or licensed may not be run if company data resides on computer or computer accesses a company network.

■ All company information and network connections must be secured (e.g. locked up before leaving work area).

■ Passwords may not be stored on employee-owned equipment, and the following security measures must be installed whenever computer is left unattended:

If networks can access a company network and the user ID or password are contained in a script file THEN a logical (software) lock must be used. IF the employee doesn't access the network, but the computer stores proprietary information THEN a logical or physical lock must be used.

Supervisors must be satisfied that these information protection safeguards are in place before authorizing employees to use their own equipment. Exceptions can be granted with management approval.

EXPENSES

REIMBURSABLE
Reimbursable expenses include:
- Business telephone calls
- Basic office supplies such as paper, pens, fax and computer paper

The Telecommuter's Agreement specifies other business expenses for which the supervisor has authorized reimbursement. For example, supervisors may approve installation of a second telephone line as a reimbursable expense. To be reimbursed for other business expenses that may arise, the employee should seek supervisory approval before incurring them.

NON-REIMBURSABLE
Non-reimbursable expenses include:
- Any costs related to remodelling and furnishing the home work space
- Commuting expenses between telecommuting work location and regular company work location
- Household expenses (e.g. heating and electricity)

PROPRIETARY INFORMATION
The company's policy on proprietary information must be followed. All proprietary information must be stored in a locked room, desk or file cabinet when left unattended. Proprietary information must be disposed of following company guidelines, or be returned to a company facility for shredding or recycling.

TERMINATION OF TELECOMMUTING ARRANGEMENT

Employees wanting to terminate a telecommuting arrangement should discuss the request with their supervisors at least 30 calendar days before the desired date. A supervisor should generally given an employee at least 30 calendar days notice before terminating a telecommuting arrangement, business needs permitting.

ELECOMMUTING AGREEMENT EXAMPLE

his agreement, effective _____, is between the Company nd _____, an employee of the Company. Except for those dditional conditions expressly imposed on Employee under this Agreement, the onditions of Employee's employment with the Company remain unchanged. This ocument does not constitute a contract of employment, either expressed or implied. t the Company, there is no fixed duration to the employment relationship. Employees an terminate their employment whenever they wish and for whatever reason they ight have, just as the Company may terminate an employee at any time for any wful reason. This is known as 'employment-at-will'.

I have read the following documents and agree to follow the policies and procedures utlined in them:

- Company telecommuting policy and related documents
- Company code of conduct, employee handbook
- Company security instructions

he location from which I will telecommute is (give full address):

_____
_____
_____
_____

ly work area at the above location will be as follows (describe room):

_____
_____
_____
_____

establishing the home work area, I have determined that all common safety ractices have been followed, and that this area provides a safe work environment r myself and others who may enter it.

My telecommuting schedule on a weekly basis will be as follows:

Day _____

Hours _____

Home office _____

Company _____

Day _____

Hours _____

Home office _____

Company _____

Day _____

Hours _____

Home office _____

Company _____

Day _____

Hours _____

Home office _____

Company _____

Day _____

Hours _____

Home office _____

Company _____

If not scheduled on a weekly basis, describe the telecommuting schedule:

_____

_____

_____

_____

During scheduled telecommuting times, I can be reached at:
_____ and, if applicable at _____

I agree to obtain my telephone messages at least _____ times on each scheduled work day while telecommuting.

Work assignments that I will work on and outputs I will produce while telecommuting are:

_____
_____
_____
_____

The Company will provide the following equipment for my telecommuting arrangement:

_____
_____
_____
_____

In addition to those listed in the Company telecommuting policy, reimbursable expenses include:

_____
_____
_____
_____

If this Agreement is part of a telecommuting trial or if the supervisor has agreed to this telecommuting agreement for a predetermined period of time, the termination date of the Agreement is _____

This Telecommuting Agreement may be terminated at any time by the supervisor provided the employee receives at least 30 days' notice before the termination date.

Employee's Signature _____

Date _____

Supervisor's Signature _____

Date _____

Supervisor's Name (Printed):

_____

Supervisor's Title

_____

Company (Department, Division, Organization)

_____

EMPLOYEE TELECOMMUTING PRE-SURVEY
The following survey has been designed to assess your expectations concerning the telecommuting program. Individual responses are confidential and will be used for statistical purposes only.

Name _____

Title _____

BU/Div. _____

Office location _____

Room# _____

State _____ Zip _____

Work Phone _____

How do you presently commute to work?

Drive alone   _____ Days a week
Carpool   _____ Days a week
Bus   _____ Days a week
Van pool   _____ Days a week
Walk   _____ Days a week
Bicycle   _____ Days a week

If you commute by car, what size car do you use?
☐ 4 cylinder   ☐ 8 cylinder
☐ 6 cylinder   ☐ Other (specify: _____)

What is the roundtrip distance from your home to your work location? _____ miles
What do you for parking at your work location? $ _____ per month
What is your normal start time at work? _____
What is your normal end time at work? _____
How many days a week do you anticipate telecommuting? _____ days per week

Indicate the equipment you currently have in your home:

	Own	Company
Computer	_____	_____
Printer	_____	_____
Modem	_____	_____
Electronic mail	_____	_____
Software	_____	_____
Fax machine	_____	_____
Speakerphone	_____	_____
Two-line phone	_____	_____
Other (please list) _____

_____

174

Do you plan to purchase any additional equipment to facilitate telecommuting?
- ☐ No
- ☐ Yes

If yes, please list _____

Do you currently have a second telephone line at home for computer or business purposes?
- ☐ No
- ☐ Yes

Do you plan to install an additional telephone line?
- ☐ No
- ☐ Yes

Do you already take work home?
(check all that apply)
- ☐ During the day
- ☐ During the evening
- ☐ During the weekend

If so, how often?
- _____ days/week
- _____ evenings/week
- _____ weekends/month

Does the idea of telecommuting make you feel uneasy or uncomfortable about getting your work finished on time?
- ☐ Not at all
- ☐ A little
- ☐ A lot

Are you concerned how, or if, the relationship might change between you and your supervisor after you begin teelcommuting?
- ☐ Not concerned at all
- ☐ A little concerned
- ☐ Very concerned

Do you think telecommuting will help you spend more time working on tasks and objectives?
- ☐ Not at all
- ☐ A little
- ☐ Much more time

What benefits do you anticipate as a result of telecommuting? (check all that apply)
- ☐ Increases in my productivity
- ☐ Improvements in my morale
- ☐ Allows me to better balance work and family responsibilities
- ☐ Avoiding stressful commute
- ☐ Other (specify: _____)

Why do you think your organization offers telecommuting? (check all that apply)
- ☐ They recognize my need for flexibility
- ☐ They are demonstrating that they care about, and want to meet, my needs
- ☐ They are environmentally-concerned about air quality and commuter trip reduction
- ☐ Other (specify: _____)

How much do you think telecommuting will favourably affect the quality of your work?
- ☐ None (remains the same)
- ☐ A little
- ☐ A lot

Do you think telecommuting will help you better manage the time you spend on your work?
- ☐ None (remains the same)
- ☐ A little
- ☐ A lot

Additional thoughts or concerns?

_____
_____
_____
_____
_____
_____
_____
_____
_____
_____
_____
_____

UPERVISORY TELECOMMUTING PRE-SURVEY

he following survey has been designated to assess your expectations concerning
e telecommuting program. Individual responses are confidential and will be used for
atistical purposes only.

ame _____
itle _____
U/Div. _____
ffice location _____
oom# _____
tate _____ Zip _____
/ork Phone _____

1. Do you feel that telecommuting has potential to benefit your organization?
   - [ ] No (skip to Q.3)
   - [ ] Yes
   - [ ] Uncertain

2. How do you feel telecommuting could benefit your organization? (check all that apply)
   - [ ] Increases staff productivity due to an improved environment with fewer interruptions
   - [ ] Increases employee efficiency due to gained ability to work at personal peak times
   - [ ] Improves employee morale
   - [ ] Assists in retaining valuable employees
   - [ ] Allows employees to balance work and family life
   - [ ] May reduce demand for office space

   How do you feel telecommuting will impact your job of supervising be employees?
   - [ ] No change
   - [ ] Supervision of telecommuters should be easier since I will be measuring performance by results
   - [ ] Supervision of telecommuters should be more difficult because

   _____
   _____
   _____
   _____

4. Would you consider purchasing new, or loaning existing equipment to employees so that they may telecommute?
   - [ ] No
   - [ ] Yes

5. Would you consider paying for the installation of a second phone line in the telecommuting employee's home?
   ☐ No
   ☐ Yes

6. Do you feel telecommuting will affect the employee's performance evaluation in any way?
   ☐ No
   ☐ Yes (specify: _____)

7. Given the opportunity, would you telecommute?
   ☐ No
   ☐ Yes

8. How many days a week would you telecommute? _____ days per week

9. How do you presently commute to work?
   Drive alone   _____ Days a week
   Carpool   _____ Days a week
   Bus   _____ Days a week
   Van pool   _____ Days a week
   Walk   _____ Days a week
   Bicycle   _____ Days a week

10. If you commute by car, what size car do you use?
    ☐ 4 cylinder
    ☐ 6 cylinder
    ☐ 8 cylinder
    ☐ Other (specify: _____)

11. How many miles per gallon does your car get? _____ mpg

12. What is the roundtrip distance from your home to your work location?
    _____ miles

13. What do you pay for parking at your work location? $ _____ per month

14. What is your normal start time at work? _____

5. What is your normal end time at work? _____

6. Indicate the equipment you currently have in your home:

	Own	Company
Computer	_____	_____
Printer	_____	_____
Modem	_____	_____
Electronic mail	_____	_____
Software	_____	_____
Fax machine	_____	_____
Speakerphone	_____	_____
Two-line phone	_____	_____
Other (please list)	_____
_____		

7. Would you plan to purchase any additional equipment to facilitate telecommuting?
   ☐ No
   ☐ Yes
   If yes, please list _____

8. Do you currently have a second telephone line at home for computer or business purposes?
   ☐ No
   ☐ Yes

9. If not, would you plan to install an additional telephone line?
   ☐ No
   ☐ Yes

10. Do you already take work home? (check all that apply)
   ☐ During the day
   ☐ During the evening
   ☐ During the weekend

11. If so, how often?
   _____ days/week
   _____ evenings/week
   _____ weekends/month

Additional thoughts or concerns?
_____
_____
_____

POST/IN PROGRESS TELECOMMUTING SURVEY FOR EMPLOYEES

This survey is designed to assess your experiences with the telecommuting program. Please take the time necessary to complete this survey so that comprehensive evaluation of the program can be made. Individual responses are confidential and will be used for program evaluation only.

Name _____

Title _____

BU/Div. _____

Office location _____

Room# _____

State _____ Zip _____

Work Phone number _____

1. How long have you worked for the company?
   _____ years _____ months

2. How long have you worked in your present position?
   _____ years _____ months

3. How do you presently commute to work?
   Drive alone   _____ Days a week
   Carpool   _____ Days a week
   Bus   _____ Days a week
   Van pool   _____ Days a week
   Walk   _____ Days a week
   Bicycle   _____ Days a week

   If you commute by car, what size car do you use?
   ☐ 4 cylinder
   ☐ 6 cylinder
   ☐ 8 cylinder
   ☐ Other (specify: _____)

   How many miles per gallon does your car get? _____ mpg

4. What is the roundtrip distance from your home to your work location?
   _____ miles

5. What do you pay for parking at your work location? $_____ per month

6. What is your normal start time at work? _____

   What is your normal end time at work? _____

7. How many minutes does it usually take to get to work? _____ minutes one way

8. How many minutes does it usually take to get home? _____ minutes one way

9. What day(s) do you normally telecommute?
   - [ ] Mon.   [ ] Thurs.
   - [ ] Tues.   [ ] Fri.
   - [ ] Wed.   [ ] No set day(s)

10. If you had a designated telecommuting day, were you able to telecommute on that day the majority of the time?
    - [ ] No
    - [ ] Yes

11. Where in your home do you usually work while telecommuting?
    - [ ] home office
    - [ ] kitchen
    - [ ] dining room
    - [ ] living room
    - [ ] other (specify: _____)

12. What type of work tasks did you do while telecommuting? (check all that apply)
    - [ ] analysing
    - [ ] editing
    - [ ] budgets
    - [ ] evaluations
    - [ ] client meetings
    - [ ] planning
    - [ ] computer work
    - [ ] project management
    - [ ] creating
    - [ ] reading
    - [ ] data base management
    - [ ] research
    - [ ] design work
    - [ ] writing

13. Is this type of work easier to do at home than in the office?
    - ☐ No
    - ☐ Yes
    - ☐ Varies

14. Have you been successful in keeping work and home separate when telecommuting?
    - ☐ No
    - ☐ Yes
    - ☐ Varies

15. Does telecommuting give you the flexibility to better balance work and family needs?
    - ☐ No
    - ☐ Yes
    - ☐ Unsure

16. What equipment/services do you use or need when telecommuting? Indicate the equipment you currently have in your home:

	Own	Co-loaned	Need
Computer	_____	_____	_____
Software	_____	_____	_____
Modem	_____	_____	_____
Electronic mail	_____	_____	_____
Printer	_____	_____	_____
Fax machine	_____	_____	_____
Second phone line	_____	_____	_____
Two-line phone	_____	_____	_____
Answering machine	_____	_____	_____
AUDIX (voice messaging)	_____	_____	_____

17. Did you need technical support from the office while telecommuting (help with computer, software, etc.)?
    - ☐ No
    - ☐ Yes

8. Did you need clerical support while telecommuting?
  - ☐ No
  - ☐ Yes, often
  - ☐ Yes, occasionally

9. While telecommuting, do you normally get your messages?
  - ☐ Call into AUDIX/Voice mail
  - ☐ Have AUDIX notify me when new messages are left
  - ☐ Have my office forward calls to my home
  - ☐ Call my clerical support
  - ☐ Other (specify: _____)

0. While telecommuting, how often do you typically call your office?
  _____ times a day

1. While telecommuting, how often do you typically receive calls from your office?
  _____ times a day

2. Has telecommuting:

	Yes	No	Not Sure
Helped you better manage your time?	_____	_____	_____
Enabled you to work at your personal peak time?	_____	_____	_____
Favourably affected the way you meet work objectives	_____	_____	_____
Given you the opportunity to plan better and be more organized	_____	_____	_____
If you've been able to plan better, has this enables you to be more productive in the office?	_____	_____	_____

3. Have you found that you experience fewer distractions while working at home?
  - ☐ No
  - ☐ Yes

4. Does your immediate family/roommates support your telecommuting activity?
  - ☐ No
  - ☐ Yes
  - ☐ Not an issue – I live alone

25. Has telecommuting affected the relationship between you and your co-workers?
    ☐ No
    ☐ Yes, positively
    ☐ Yes, negatively

26. If yes, how has your relationship been affected?

    _____
    _____
    _____

27. Do any of your co-workers resent the fact that you telecommute?
    ☐ Yes, a great deal
    ☐ Yes, somewhat
    ☐ No, not at all
    ☐ Not sure

28. While telecommuting, do you miss the social interaction of the office?
    ☐ Never
    ☐ A little
    ☐ A lot
    ☐ Not sure

29. Has telecommuting affected the relationship between you and your supervisor?
    ☐ No
    ☐ Yes, positively
    ☐ Yes, negatively

30. If yes, how has your relationship been affected?

    _____
    _____
    _____

31. Has your supervisor shown more or less confidence in you since you've been telecommuting?
    ☐ More confidence
    ☐ No change
    ☐ Less confidence
    ☐ Not sure

2. Does your supervisor telecommute?
   - ☐ No
   - ☐ Yes

3. If yes, how has this affected you?

_____

_____

_____

4. Have you felt guilty about having the opportunity to work at home?
   - ☐ Not at all
   - ☐ A little
   - ☐ A lot
   - ☐ Not sure

5. What is your present attitude toward telecommuting?
   - ☐ Positive
   - ☐ Somewhat positive
   - ☐ Neutral
   - ☐ Somewhat negative
   - ☐ Negative

6. Have your expectations of telecommuting matched the realities of working at home?
   - ☐ No
   - ☐ Yes

7. If no, why not?

_____

_____

_____

8. If given a choice, would you rather spend more, less or the same amount of time telecommuting?
   - ☐ More time
   - ☐ The same amount of time
   - ☐ Less time

9. If less time, why?

_____

_____

_____

40. Has your attitude toward your present job changed since you've been given the opportunity to work at home?
☐ Greatly improved
☐ Slightly improved
☐ Remained the same
☐ Slightly worse
☐ Much worse

41. In future career choices, would the option of telecommuting affect your decision?
☐ Yes, I would prefer to telecommute
☐ Yes, I would prefer NOT to telecommute
☐ No, it would not affect my decision

42. Has having the opportunity to telecommute shown you that: (check all that apply)
☐ Your organization empowers you
☐ Your organization trusts you
☐ Your organization cares about your need to balance your work and family needs

43. Has telecommuting provided you with benefits that you haven't already mentioned?
_____
_____
_____

44. Have you encountered any problems while working at home that you haven't already mentioned?
_____
_____
_____

45. What would you do to enhance the telecommuting program?
_____
_____
_____

46. Would you recommend telecommuting to other employees?
☐ No
☐ Yes
☐ Not sure

POST-TELECOMMUTING SUPERVISOR SURVEY
This survey is designed to assess your experiences with the telecommuting program. The questionnaire is divided into two sections, short answer and essay answer. Please take the time necessary to complete this survey so that comprehensive evaluation of the program can be made. Individual responses are confidential and will be used for program evaluation only.

Name _____

Title _____

BU/Div. _____

Office location _____

Work Phone number _____

PART I (to be completed by all supervisors of telecommuters)

1. How many employees do you supervise? _____ employees

2. How many of your employees are telecommuting? _____ telecommuters

3. Did your relationship with your telecommuting employees changes as a result of their telecommuting?
   ☐ No, it stayed the same
   ☐ Yes, it improved
   ☐ Yes, it got worse

4. Has the trust and confidence you have in your telecommuting employees been affected?
   ☐ Yes, favourably
   ☐ No change
   ☐ Yes, unfavourably

5. How has telecommuting affected:
   a. the quality of telecommuter's work?
   ☐ Substantially improved
   ☐ Slightly improved
   ☐ Remained the same
   ☐ Slightly decreased
   ☐ Greatly decreased
   b. the quantity of work accomplished by the telecommuter?
   ☐ Substantially increased
   ☐ Slightly increased
   ☐ Remained the same
   ☐ Slightly decreased
   ☐ Greatly decreased

c. the overall productivity of your organization?
- ☐ Substantially increased
- ☐ Slightly increased
- ☐ Remained the same
- ☐ Slightly decreased
- ☐ Greatly decreased

d. your work load?
- ☐ Substantially increased
- ☐ Slightly increased
- ☐ Remained the same
- ☐ Slightly decreased
- ☐ Greatly decreased

6. Did you find it necessary to better define work products for your telecommuters?
- ☐ No
- ☐ Yes

If yes, did you benefit from this?
- ☐ No
- ☐ Yes
- ☐ Can't tell yet

7. Did you find more frequent meetings were necessary to ensure progress of assignments of telecommuters?
- ☐ No
- ☐ Yes
- ☐ Not sure

8. Has telecommuting made it easier for your telecommuters to meet work objectives?
- ☐ No
- ☐ Yes
- ☐ Not sure

9. Was it easier to assess goals and objectives because you had to concentrate on management by results?
- ☐ No
- ☐ Yes
- ☐ Not sure

0. Was the telecommuting agreement a helpful tool for you in outlining clear expectations with your telecommuter?
   - ☐ No
   - ☐ Yes
   - ☐ Not sure

1. How did telecommuting affect the employee's appraisal?
   - ☐ Made easier
   - ☐ No effect
   - ☐ Made harder
   - ☐ Unknown

2. Did you find your employees needed additional equipment/services in order to effectively telecommute?
   - ☐ No
   - ☐ Yes

   If yes, what type of equipment/services did they need?

   _____
   _____
   _____

   Did your organization: (check that all apply)
   - ☐ Loan needed equipment to the telecommuter
   - ☐ Purchase needed equipment/services for the telecommuter
   - ☐ Ask the employee to purchase their own equipment/services
   - ☐ Ask the employee to pick up some costs, and the organization picked up other costs

   Approximately, what did your organization pay to purchase new equipment/services?
   $ _____ per telecommuter
   $ _____ in total

3. Was it difficult to hold group meetings because of the telecommuting schedules of your employees?
   - ☐ No
   - ☐ Yes

4. Did you have problems dealing with employees that were not allowed to telecommute?
   - ☐ No
   - ☐ Yes
   - ☐ Not applicable

If yes, what did you encounter?

_____

_____

_____

15. Do you want employees to continue telecommuting?
    ☐ No
    ☐ Yes
    ☐ Varies with employees
    ☐ Not sure

16. Would you be willing to allow more of your employees to telecommute?
    ☐ No
    ☐ Yes
    ☐ Some yes, some no
    ☐ Not applicable, all telecommute

17. Do you telecommute?
    ☐ No
    ☐ Yes

    If no, would you like to?
    ☐ No
    ☐ Yes
    ☐ Not sure

    If yes, why haven't you?

_____

_____

_____

18. Results from the pre-telecommuting surveys show that supervisors thought tele-commuting had the potential to benefit their organization in a variety of ways. Please indicate whether you think the benefits listed below have been demonstrated by writing one of the following letter before each response:
    A – Strongly demonstrated
    B – Demonstrated somewhat
    C – Did not demonstrate

_____ Telecommuting allows employees to balance work and family life
_____ Telecommuting assists in retaining valuable employees
_____ Telecommuting provides reduction in air pollution, traffic, stress, miles
driven and travel time
_____ Telecommuting increased the worker(s) productivity
_____ Telecommuting did not interfere with worker(s) productivity
_____ Telecommuting improved employee morale
_____ Telecommuting did not affect non-telecommuting employee morale

9. Do you have additional comments or concerns you should like to express?

_____
_____
_____
_____
_____
_____
_____
_____
_____
_____

PART 11
(to be completed by all supervisors who telecommute)

. Have your areas of responsibilities benefited from the fact that you telecommute?
☐ No
☐ Yes

If yes, how?

_____
_____
_____

. Was your immediate supervisor impacted on the days you telecommute?
☐ No
☐ Yes

If yes, how?

_____
_____
_____

3. As a telecommuting supervisor, did you have adequate communications with your staff?

☐ No
☐ Yes

If yes, how?

_____

_____

_____

4. Would you encourage other supervisors to telecommute?

☐ No
☐ Yes
☐ Not sure

13 EU study on teleworking

Telework in Europe is advanced in some countries and lagging behind in others. This 1995 summary of the Penetration, Potential and Practice study for the European Union by Werner Korte of empirica in Germany and Richard Wynne of Work Research Centre in Ireland shows better than anything else available where Europe stands in the introduction of home-based working at least as far as government sponsoring encouragement and understanding is concerned.

Conditions for Telework Development

An important part of the TELDET project's work related to assessing the position, activities and policies of major stakeholders towards telework. The results of the work of this project strand on the assessment of telework stimulation policies are the crucial third element of assessing the prospects of teleworking in the future.

The information gathered in this line of work provides an overview of the conditions for the development of telework in the majority of the EU countries (Belgium, Denmark, Finland, France, Germany, Greece, Ireland, Italy, the Netherlands, Portugal, Spain and the United Kingdom). Where possible it differentiates between national, regional and municipal level activities and programmes and those of the national PTTs and telecommunications network providers. It focuses on policies which more or less directly deal with the subject of telework and had or are likely to have an impact on the development of telework. The information provided refers to the situation in each country in the beginning of 1995. This material for this chapter has been taken from a longer report which is available from the TELDET partners.

In this format it integrates for the first time and in a single source information which can be used by politicians and decision makers all over Europe to support their strategies, activities and policies to telework.

Belgium

To assess the conditions for development of telework in Belgium is not easy because, even if interest in telework is evident and if some initiatives exist, there is not a clear strategy defined at either national or regional levels.

Four initiatives have been identified as a result of work in the TELDET project:

1 A study has been undertaken by the Verbond van Kristelijke Werkgevers en Kaderleden, a Flemish Christian employers association on the conditions of development for telework. Two brochures were published in 1992 and 1993, as a result of the study. The first focused on the legal, tax, social and economic aspects of telework and the main advantages of telework for a company. The second describes nine telework schemes in Belgium, most of them at the pilot or early stage of development.

2 The second initiative is that of the Belgian Teleworking Association. Created in May 1994, the Association aims to study, promote and assist in the implementation of all forms of telework in Belgium. The activities and services of the association are based on:

- A newsletter publishing information from Belgium and abroad
- Fact sheets explaining various facets of teleworking such as setting up a home office, legal issues or telecommunications
- Market studies
- Education and training programmes ranging from awareness programmes to sessions on implementing telework
- Events such as lunch-time debates and regional and national conferences
- Special interest groups
- An electronic library hosted by the ECTF Forum on CompuServe
- A help desk
- A secretariat.

194

3   An initiative has been started by the Ministry of Labour
    and Employment concerning the status of teleworkers.
    This work is in progress and should give recommenda-
    tions in 1995.
4   The last initiative is located in the Euro-Region Meuse-
    Rhin which covers regions from Germany, Belgium and
    The Netherlands. A global study on regional development
    was carried out. Telematics were considered as part of
    this study.

Denmark

In general, the concept of teleworking has not been given
any real consideration in Denmark. Currently, there is no
formal policy on telework or the related use of information
technology in work arrangements at a national or regional
level. Where telework initiatives exist, they are usually informal arrangements between employers and employees.

In the early 1980s, the Danish government provided
funding for the setting up of Teleservice centres or
Telecottages to provide information and services to remote
communities. These centres have played a major part in
bringing computer knowledge and skills to a large number
of people, through training courses and workshops. At
present the Telecottages are still regarded as a social
experiment although new centres are continually being set
up, many of them in remote areas. As in many other
European countries, Telecottages have succeeded in bringing an awareness and knowledge of IT to local communities but they have not succeeded in bringing telework
opportunities.

While the Danish government has no explicit policy on
telework, it has been active in conducting IT research for a
number of years. Teleworking issues have formed a very
little part of this research programme.

Denmark has both the human and technical resources to
exploit teleworking. The Danish telecommunications infrastructure is very well developed with 265 out of 275 munic-
ipalities linked up to the national broadband network. In
addition, 26% of all homes are equipped with a computer
and 85% of all white collar workers use a computer on a
daily basis. More generally, the Danish workforce is well
educated with a large number of experienced IT-users who
are also familiar with telecommunications.

A number of factors may hinder the development of teleworking in Denmark, one of the main ones being the cost of phone calls and data transmission, despite their being among the lowest in Europe. Another major factor which may deter the development of teleworking is the way this form of work is perceived to conflict with the traditional management methods used in many Danish companies.

One sector where official policy on information technology does exist is in education – policy requires teachers in all parts of the educational system to stimulate the use of technology. The national phone company, TeleDenmark, and the Ministry of Education are engaged in a new initiative in this area. They have set up a project which aims to provide every Danish educational institution with a network facility similar to the Internet. The intention is to provide on-line communication with colleagues and students as well as with public and private sector organizations.

Finland

Most of the numerous telework stimulation activities in Finland aim to promote regional development, especially in relation to job creation and training of people living in rural areas. This emphasis is a natural consequence of the real needs of rural areas. This policy has perhaps led to a lack of action at urban level, though there are now initial telework schemes being undertaken by the private sector in urban areas. Private companies and people living in urban areas in the context of organizational development, business restructuring and local service provision.

The spread of telematic systems and telework arrangements has been encouraged by key players such as the Ministry of Labour, Finnish Telecom, the Technology Development Centre (TEKES), National Research & Development Centre for Welfare and Health (STAKES), the Finnish Flexiwork Forum, the University of Turku, the Helsinki University of Technology and the Finnish Association of Telecottages (FITEC). So far, the efforts of these agencies towards telework development have not been coordinated.

The first national level activities in promoting the diffusion of telework in Finland began at the end of the 1980s, when the Ministry of Social Affairs and Health set up a committee to clarify the advantages and disadvantages of homework and telework and to weigh their implications for legislation. The committee concluded that telework is a useful phenomenon, which promotes improvements in both productivity and quality of working life. This committee saw no need to introduce special legal arrangements.

Concurrent with activities of the committee, the first experimental projects and studies on teleworking were launched at regional and municipal level, in the counties of North-Karelia and Paijat-Hame. In these pioneering projects emphasis was put on strengthening local communities and using telecommuting possibilities. The revitalization of villages in remote areas has been a dominating theme in the discussion of the possibilities of telework since that time, perhaps to the exclusion of investigation into the broader opportunities which telework offers for both business and the worker.

Despite these potential shortcomings, it is recognized that telework is a prominent tool in rural policy. Good examples include the projects taking place in North-Karelia and Turku archipelago. Several current Finnish telework initiatives will come under the aegis of the European Social Fund in 1995.

Telework policy in Finland is defined in the report of the theme group on telework set up by the Ministry of the Interior. The emphasis of telework policy is shifting towards the promotion of networking, and other practical applications both on an organizational level and in local communities due to this report. Technology-pushed or otherwise biased and unrealistic applications of telework will slowly give way to customer-oriented and practical approaches.

France

Defining the kinds of telework which currently exist in France is necessary to understand how teleworking is promoted and how conditions for its development are set up. Teleworking in France can be categorized into three types:

1 Telecommuting
2 Tele-deployment – either offshore or inshore
3 Teleservices, commercial teleservices and non-commercial teleservices, i.e. for the general public.

Perhaps the main actor in relation to teleworking in France is DATAR (a governmental organization responsible for regional development). DATAR contracted a team of experts to visit the Philippines, the United States, Ireland, South Africa, Mauritius, La Reunion, Japan and China on a fact-finding mission, which led to a clearly defined national level strategy to promote the development of telework in France. The strategy was based on:

1 The emergence of the tele-economy as a key driving force for the advancement of society
2 Regional development considerations.

The emergence of the tele-economy has created a new international division of labour and an increasing globalization of markets. Immaterial activities have been identified as the main added-value element in the process of production of goods or services (the immaterial aspect is concerned with the fact that products do not have a physical existence). Telework and teleservices generally, therefore, can become a major tool of regional development policy.

The tele-economy is based on the globalization of services taking advantage of labour costs, tax, profit taxation, but it also has consequences at the regional level. Teleservices providers in regions are growing considerably and a large number of companies are interested in outsourcing part of their processes of production and administrative tasks.

The French response to this challenge is based on the three DATAR calls for projects, launched successively since 1990 with the aim of sensitizing the major socio-economic actors to this new environment and the current initiatives concerning the information society which will lead to the launch of pilots all over France to test the economic and technical feasibility of telematics applications and services and patterns of usage.

The three DATAR projects were:

1 New Information and Communication Technologies and Innovative Projects dealing with Regional Development (1990)
2 The 1992 call deals directly with telework, linking national and regional development with economic competitiveness
3 The 1993 call considers telework and employment in the context of regional development.

EU study on teleworking

As a result of the three calls for projects, 257 projects were selected and supported, of which:

1   25% were dedicated to non-commercial services such as training, education, administrative information and services, environment, healthcare, and social care services.
2   75% were dedicated to commercial services which contribute to a new organization of labour and organizations – telemaintenance, tele-assistance, tele-marketing, deployment of activities, reinforcement of export activities.

As a result of these initiatives more than 3000 jobs were created, deployed maintained or regenerated.

Other activities include a 1994 report for the Ministry for Enterprise on teleservices in France. The report – 'Teleservices in France; which markets for the information highways' – produced an assessment of the potential size of the sector to the years 2000 and 2005. Teleservices include all added-value services both of companies and the general public which can be provided remotely through the use of telecommunication.

The current market was assessed at 33 billion FF in 1993 and the report describes two scenarios for the growth of the sector in the next 10 years. The pessimistic scenario estimates growth at 8.6% per year whereas the optimistic scenario estimates annual growth at 16%.

French organizations have been active in the 4th Framework Programme within the ACTS and Telematics initiatives, as well as the initiative taken by the DGXIII and DGXVI of networking six European regions, (Nord-Pas de Calais is one of the regions). These projects are expected to have A significant impact on promoting teleworking and teleservices projects.

Beyond these programmes, two new initiatives at the national level will strengthen the development of telematics, telework and teleservices:

1   The call for tender for testing new services on the information highways managed by the Ministry of Industry, Posts and Telecommunication and International Trade. This initiative focuses on two action lines – services and

platforms. The first deals with rapid testing of new commercial or public services which take advantage of the information highway. The second deals with implementing technical platforms which provide the advanced functionalities needed to develop and test new services.

2 The call for Projects on digital sites managed by DATAR. A digital site is a geographic area in which people can access simultaneously integrated services, be they commercial or non-commercial.

In conclusion, it is evident that national initiatives play a major role in promoting telework and teleservices in France. Regional level actions or initiatives also exist, for example in Aquitaine, Centre, Corsica, Ile de France, Languedoc-Roussillon, Lorraine, Midi-Pyrenées, Nord-Pas de Calais, Picardie, Provence-Alps-Cóte d'Azur and Rhóne-Alps but these are closely related to national actions.

Germany

Programmes and activities aimed at the stimulation of telework have up until recently been rather scarce in Germany. At a Federal level these started in the mid- to late-1980s when the Federal Ministry of Regional Development, Housing and City Planning commissioned research projects in the area of the impact of new IT&T on regions. Partly as a consequence (though there was some prior activity), a larger number of telehouses have been established in different, mainly rural areas in Germany. However, the German telehouses have not been successful in establishing teleworking, opportunities none offer teleservices as part of their activities. Most have developed into organizations – still using public funds – offering IT-related training courses, conferences, etc. Another expression of the mixed experiences of telehouses is the termination of the public funding of the German Telecottages Association.

The Federal Ministry of Research and Technology (BMFT) has in 1994 begun a large R&D program entitled 'Telecooperation". This seeks to develop, implement and use co-operative telecommunications systems in public administrations and industrial organizations. One focus of these projects is on the support of distributed co-operative working between public authorities in Berlin and Bonn by means of multifunctional systems and sophisticated

telecommunications networks and services. It is expected that these projects where the application of telework-related IT&T will be demonstrated in real work environments will help stimulate the development of telework.

The Ministry of Post and Telecommunications (the predecessor of Deutsche Telekom AG) did not develop any activities in the area of telework until the late 1980s. The situation changed when Deutsche Telekom AG developed their general teleworking strategy in 1993/94. They now aim to establish a number of company internal pilot projects. In addition the Anwenderforum Telekommunikation (AFT) of Deutsche Telekom AG established a working group on telework at the end of 1994 which consists of a number of companies. This working group aims to define telework-related requirements for telecommunications networks and services and to develop an approach to raising awareness of and introducing telework to enterprises.

In parallel to the Federal activities, a number of Lander ministries began R&D projects and studied in the area of telework in the mid- to late 1980s. These mainly aimed to identify the opportunities and threats of this new form of work organization – mainly for women – as it is believed that these would become the major target group of telework. An early teleworking experiment was funded by the Federal State Baden-Wurttemberg in 1984. However, it did not spur further interest in this subject among companies at this time, largely because of the technological problems with quite expensive and significantly less sophisticated and powerful IT&T which then had to be used.

A few Federal State governments and ministries have started or are about to start their own programmes and activities in the area of application of IT&T, which include telework. Northrhine Westphalia started in the late 1980s with its Teletech Initiative funded by the Ministry of Economic Affairs and Technology. Having completed a study on the potential for telework in SMEs, the Teletech Initiative is currently discussing the establishment of a telework competence centre. The same ministry is currently (1995) establishing a new programme in this area called media NRW (NRW stands for Northrhine-Westphalia) in which telework constitutes one important area for demonstration projects.

Bavaria has carried out a programme where it developed a concept for and offered alternative teleworking opportunities to young farmers to become CAD/CAM designers offering their services as teleworkers on the market. This programme running from 1990 to 1993 had not yielded the expected results as only a very small number of farmers have been successful. Recently, the Bavarian Ministry of Agriculture and Nutrition has assigned a budget to fund telework projects in rural areas. A first pilot project has just started. Also the Bavarian Ministry of Economic Affairs and Traffic has started the preparation of a programme on telematics and telework applications by setting up working groups of experts to define such a programme. First work group meetings took place in autumn 1994 and the programme called 'Bayern Online' is presently being shaped.

Baden-Wurttemberg has started a programme called 'Pilot Project Multimedia Baden-Wurttemberg'. The aim of this programme is the experimentation with and usability analysis of multimedia communications services for private households and SMEs. Its budget is around 100 million DM and they are currently discussing whether telework experiments should become part of the programme.

Berlin is currently developing a programme aimed at the development and establishment of viable IT&T application pilot projects including those demonstrating different forms of teleworking.

Greece

The conditions for teleworking in Greece are, as yet, not highly developed. There are no major initiatives or teleworking schemes which are promoted at a national level. In addition, the availability of advanced telecommunications infrastructure is low – Greek Telecom does not as yet offer ISDN services, for example.

However, a number of initiatives regarding the integration of disabled people through teleworking or tele-education are underway. These projects include TWIN, which seeks to develop international networking between telecentres for the disabled, TELED – a Horizon initiative offering higher education for the disabled via telematics, TELEWORKING – a project employing disabled people who offer telematics advice to SMEs via telematics and TELEGREAT – a distance training and job placement initiative by a regional centre of the rehabilitation of disabled people.

Ireland

On a national level, there is no explicit public policy regarding the development of teleworking in Ireland and experience of teleworking to date have generally been limited to back-office and satellite or offshore activity. There is very little awareness of the concept among government departments, employer bodies, trade unions and indeed among the general public. As a consequence hardly any research is being undertaken into its feasibility.

There are, however, a number of actions which have served to stimulate a limited range of teleworking activities and some of these are quite large in scale. The development of the telecommunications infrastructure, under the STAR programme of the EU, along with the government policy on telecommunications pricing have modernized Irish telecommunications and introduced very competitive prices particularly in relation to international trade.

In addition, government policy on job creation identified telemarketing and telephone technical support as one of its major target sectors for development and job creation. In conjuction with the Industrial Development Authority, a three-year plan was implemented at the end of 1992 to create 2000 jobs in these areas. To date, this programme is running ahead of target, with more than 16 internationally traded service companies using satellite offices to provide offshore telemarketing and teleservices.

Government is also engaged in a programme to decentralize sections of a number of government departments to rural areas. While the primary aim of this programme is economic revitalization of these areas, the project was undertaken in tandem with the implementation of the Government Telecommunications Network (GTN). The GTN uses 2Mb leased lines and microwave links to provide remote access to and from rural offices. The network, which is not presently fully operational, will support a range of IT initiatives which will make the delivery of government services more efficient and cost effective. To date, 2800 civil servants have been relocated under this programme with a further 1000 relocations planned.

Telecom Eireann, the sole domestic telecommunications operator, are involved in the continuous development of the telecommunications infrastructure (there is a small level of competition in the area of business international calls). At present, more than 65% of exchanges have been digitized and they are currently engaged in upgrading all city exchanges to ISDN. Further reductions on both international and national telecommunication costs are planned for 1995 and beyond (current international telephone call costs are among the cheapest in the EU). While they are not directly involved in any teleworking activities they do, however, offer technical support and assistance to people setting up teleworking projects.

At a regional level, a number of teleworking initiatives have been developed with financial assistance from various EU programmes such as Telematique, Leader and NOW. Udaras na Gaeltachta, the government agency charged with economic, social and cultural development of the Gaeltachts (Irish-speaking areas – largely rural) has no formal policy on teleworking. However, it has provided grant aid and techni-cal advice to telecottage type initiatives which have set up in rural areas. As in most European countries, telecottages in Ireland have succeeded in bringing an awareness of IT&T to rural areas but the majority have not managed to secure a sufficient level of commercial contracts and function predominantly as training and service centres. However, they have also supported the establishment of telecentres which act as a breeding ground for small telecommunica-tions and IT based businesses in two locations. These have been moderately successful to date.

Italy

Italy, unlike other industralized countries, is late in introduc-ing new technical and organizational ways of working and there are still very few experiences of teleworking. Nevertheless, telework has been and is currently a matter of great interest. Since the mid-1980s major studies on telework have been carried out at a theoretical level and there has been widespread dissemination of articles published in magazines and newspapers regarding telework.

So far, the practical experiences of telework in Italy mainly involve software enterprises, and the financial, insurance and consultancy sectors. In these sectors there is a signifi-cant number of leading companies that have carried out telework schemes, e.g. the Olivetti Group, Italsiel (the leading Italian firm in information technology services), Credito Emiliano (CREDEM) in the banking sector, RAS (Riunione Adriatica di Sicurta) in the insurance sector,

O'Group and O. Dati Consulenza (consulting companies in information systems), SIP of Torino (personnel services) and SOLCO (welfare service co-operatives).

Trade unions play a significant role with regard to the regulation of the labour market – their policies in relation to teleworking have seen the maintenance of all major conditions of work for their members. A good example of this role occurred in relation to Law 300 of 1970 of the Statute of Labourers which guarantees unfair dismissal rights to employees in enterprises with more than 15 workers. This stance has militated against the development of telework.

In addition, the high cost of hardware, software and telecommunications tariffs also act as a barrier or telework development.

Notwithstanding these factors, a number of trends indicate that the situation may be changing:

1   The cultural change imposed on Italian entrepreneurs, due to the crisis of the past two years, and the need for higher competitiveness in both the European and world markets.
2   The awareness of Italian unions of the need to find innovative solutions to the problems of high labour costs and increasing unemployment.
3   The merging of the telecommunications sector into one structure, and its future privatization; as well as the deregulation by 1988 of phone-data services imposed by the European Commission.

Other factors of importance in Italy include the coming to market of IT products aimed at the mass market, in particular portable computers (note-books), easily usable applications, the telecomms operators' expanding their telematics services, (enabled by the change from analogue to digital infrastructure), and the growing unemployment crisis.

In addition, the policies undertaken at European level to stimulate regional technological development and for the facilitation of the applied research in the telematics field have acted as a further enabling factor. Among the most important European initiatives which helped develop new expectations for telework in Italy are, for example, the TELEMATIQUE, LEADER, LIFE and TSA (Telework Stimulation Action) programmes.

Teleworking

Portugal

The development of telework among Portuguese firms is limited, but there is a trend towards subcontracting some activities which could be undertaken via teleworking. many SMEs sub-contract their accounting to external companies, generally small enterprises or self-employed.

Portugal Telecom have created a set of Advanced Communication Centres located in the major urban areas, where telecommunication services such as videoconferencing are available. They have also set up rural Telecentres which allow access to facilities for information processing and communication.

Spain

Teleworking is less prevalent in Spain compared to other European countries, but it is expected that telework will increase as a result of government policies, the reformation of the labour market and the competitive environment in the field of information and telecommunication services.

The Spanish government has recently grasped the nature of the challenge presented and the strategic importance of telework. Regional governments also seem to be interested in telework development, but there is not a clear regional policy to foster telework and so far telework activities have been at a low level, with the possible exception of the Balearic Islands.

At a national level, the first telework stimulation actions begun in the early 1990s. Within the National Telecommunications Plan and with the financial support of Star and Telematique Programmes, several initiatives and projects dealing with the use of advanced communication services and telework have been set up. The implementation of CAD/CAM systems in 'shared resources centres' has allowed many industrial SMEs (textile, metallurgy, toy and glass sectors) to start teleworking. In addition, projects in the area of telemanagement services for co-operative companies, telecontrol services in several water supply companies and a project of Teleeducation created by the Telecommunication Engineering School (ETSIT) in Madrid have been implemented.

More recently, the Ministry of Transport and Telecommunications, through its Telecommunication Directorate, have developed an Action Plan for the stimulation of telework

in Spain with reference to the areas of potential major socio-economic impact. The Action Plan seeks to create a partnership between the public and private sectors, whereby the Government puts its policy weight behind the potential of telework, while the private sector is involved in financing. It also seeks to promote applications which are demand led rather than technology led, and to involve potent user beneficiaries in developing the telework market in Spain.

United Kingdom
Martlesham enables BT to offer 'Video-on-demand' to the public. This entails compressing picture signals and sending them down ordinary twisted copper pair wires – the old fashioned telephone network. The publicity generated by this service is accelerating teleworking interest.

Discussion
Teleworking has now become a major area of interest and commitment in Europe and this trend is expected to consolidate in the coming years. The changes in economic and political conditions as well as the new technological paradigm facilitate new forms of working, in the framework of the emerging Information Society.

Despite these favourable trends in most of the EU countries, the spread of telework has been relatively slow. Telework in Europe may still have to prove itself to be a sufficiently attractive economic option for companies for it to develop further.

The future success of telework will depend on a number of factors. These include the economic pressures that push the public and private enterprises to introduce flexible labour policies and to reduce fixed costs, the raising of public awareness about telework, the further spread of advanced telecommunications facilities, reductions in telecommunications costs, and the further development of social policies by both government and the private sector.

In this context, an important lesson to be learnt from current experiences is that the development of telework is not directly linked to public promotion. In most European countries, government support to more flexible ways of working has proved to be an important but not sufficient condition for telework development. On the other hand although specific teleworking policies do not exist many

Teleworking

European governments are facilitating the prospects for telework through promoting IT&T development, which has become an essential tool for the success of telework schemes.

Telework actions have often been linked to regional development policies and more specifically to job creation and training of people in rural areas. These experiences have been quite successful in Finland and France, where telework and teleservices play an important role in regional and rural development policy.

In other countries such as Denmark, Ireland, Germany or the UK, teleservices centres or telehouses/telecottages type initiatives have been set up mainly in rural and remote areas. Although they have succeeded in bringing an awareness and knowledge of IT to local communities, their contribution to the development of telework has been rather limited.

14 Telework resource list

ACRE
Somerford Court
Somerford Road
Cirencester
Gloucestershire GL7 1TW
UK
Tel: +44 1285 653477
Fax: +44 1285 654537

Adaptation Limited
Rathgar House
237 Baring Road
Grove Park London SE12 0BE
Tel: + 44 181 857 5907
Fax: +44 181 857 5947

Analytica
46 Ferntower Road
London N5 2JH
UK
Tel: +44 171 226 8411
Fax: +44 171 226 0813
E-mail: analytica@dial.pipex.com
WWW: http://dspace.dial.pipex.xom/analytica

Arizona Department of Administration
Travel Reduction Program
1700 West Washington
Suite B-52
Phoenix, Arizona 85007
USA
Tel: +1 602 542 3637
Fax: +1 602 542 3636
E-mail: JCORBETT@AD.STATE.AZ.US

Teleworking

AT&T
1945 Chaussée de Wavre
B-1160 Brussels
Belgium
Tel: +32 2 676 35 11
Fax: +32 2 676 35 04

John Willy Bakke
Telenor Research
PO Box 83
N-2007 Kjeller
Norway
Tel: +47 63 84 83 62
Fax: + 47 63 81 00 76
E-mail: john.bakke@fou.telenor.no

Bay Area Telecommuting Assistance Project
c/o ABAG
PO Box 2050
Oakland, CA 94604-2050
USA
Fax: +1 510 464 7970

Belgian TeleWorking Association
Bevrijdingslaan 5
B-1932 Sint Stevens Woluwe
Belgium
Tel: +32 2 720 30 05
Fax: +32 2 720 47 90
E-mail: 100037.357@compuserve.com

Jane Berry
WREN Telecottage
Stoneleigh Park
Warwickshire CV8 2RR
UK
Tel: +441203 696 986
Fax: +44 1203 696538
E-mail: 100114.2366@compuserve.com or
WREN@midnet.com

Telework resource list

Imogen Bertin
Cork Teleworking Centre
Reagrove
Minane Bridge
Co. Cork
Ireland
Tel: +353 21 887300
Fax: + 353 21 887 402
E-mail: 100272.1427@compuserve.com

Kathie Blankenship
Smart Valley Inc.
2520 Mission College
Santa Clara CA 95054
USA
Tel: +1 408 562 7795
Fax: +1 408 562 7677
E-mail: kathieb@svi.org

David Brain
Systems Synthesis Ltd
Waterloo House
Waterloo Street
Clifton
Bristol BS8 4BT
UK
Tel: +44 117 923 8853
Fax: +44 117 923 88 34
E-mail: info@ssynth.demon.co.uk

Brameur Ltd
Clark House
King's Road
Fleet
Hampshire GU13 9AD
Tel: +44 1252 812252
Fax: +44 1252 815702
E-mail: 100142.31@compuserve.com

Teleworking

Bridgewater Research Group NL
Aalbekerweg 67d
NL-6336 XN Hulsberg
The Netherlands
Tel: +31 45 405 2865
Fax: +31 45 405 9245
E-mail: 72261.526@compuserve.com

British Telecommunications plc
c/o Paul Maguire
Quentin Bell Organization
22 Endell Street
Covent Garden
London WC2H 9AD
UK
Tel: + 44 171 379 0304
Fax: + 44 171 497 2533

Eric Britton
EcoPlan International
Centre for Technology & Systems Studies
10 Rue Joseph Bara
F-75006 Paris
France
Tel: +33 1 4326 13 23
Fax: +33 1 43 26 07 46
E-mail: 100336.2154@compuserve.com
WWW: http://www.the-commons.org/

Caltrans – Right of Way
PO Box 85406
San Diego CA 92106
Tel: +1 619 688 6907
E-mail: CVanWans@TRMX3.DOT.CA.GOV

Centre for Rural Studies
Royal Agricultural College
Cirencester GL7 6JS
UK

Telework resource list

Sophie Chalmers
Editor, Home Run Newsletter
Active Information
Cribau Mill
Llanvair Discoed
Chepstow
Gwent NP6 6RD
UK
Tel: +44 1291 641 222
Fax: +44 1291 641 777
E-mail: 100117.27@compuserve.com

Chase Plaza Telecommuting Centre
Tel: +1 405 749 9782
Fax: +1 405 749 8516
E-mail: kurt.mcdaniel@gsa.gov

David Child
TeleTeam Ltd
17 Shannon Close
Grove OX12 7PT
Tel: +44 831 332888 or +44 589 083842
Fax: +44 1235 766568
E-mail: 100112.323@compuserve.com

City of Modesto
Community Development Department
801 11th Street
PO Box 642
Modesto CA 95353
USA
Tel: + 1 209 571 5566
Fax: + 1 209 571 5128

Peter Claffey
Deputy Chief Inspector
Health & Safety Authority
10 Hogan Place
Dublin 2, Ireland
Tel: +353 1 662 0400
Fax: +353 1 662 0417
E-mail: pjc@hsa.ie
WWW: http://www.hsa.ie/osh

Teleworking

Ann Collins
Proto-Type
Spinney House
Compasses Road
Pattiswick
Essex CM7 8BG
UK
Tel: +44 1376 561 010
Fax: +44 1376 562 899
E-mail: 101665.405@compuserve.com

Commission of the European Communities
DG XIII
Rue de la Loi 200
B-1049 Brussels
Belgium
Tel: + 32 2 299 11 11
Fax: +32 2 296 88 80

Susan Coulson-Thomas
Adaptation Ltd
Rathgar House
237 Baring Road
Grove Park London SE12 0BE
Tel: + 44 181 857 5907
Fax: +44 181 857 5947

Ian Culpin
DGXIII-B
Rue de la Loi 200
B-1049 Brussels
Belgium
Tel: + 32 2 295 9054
Fax: + 32 2 296 17 86
E-mail: 100037.357@compuserve.com

The Data Protection Registrar
Wycliffe House
Water Lane
Wilmslow
Cheshire SK9 5AF
UK
Tel: +44 1625 545745
Fax: +44 1625 524 510
E-mail: data@wycliffe.demon.co.uk

Telework resource list

Scott Decker
Puget Sound Telecommuting Demonstration
Washington State Energy Office
925 Plum St SE
Bldg 4
PO Box 43165
Olympia WA 98504-3165
USA
Tel: +1 360 956 2055
Fax: +1 360 956 2218
E-mail: scodec@wseo.wa.gov

Alan Denbigh
Executive Director
The Telecottage Association
Wren Telecottage
Stoneleigh Park
Warwickshire CV8 2RR
UK
Tel: +44 1203 696 986
Fax: +44 1203 696 538
E-mail: 100114.2366@compuserve.com

Durham University Business School
Knowledge Systems Research Centre
Mill Hill Lane
Durham City DH1 3LB
UK
Tel: +44 191 374 2211
Fax: +44 191 374 3748
E-mail Ted.Fuller@durham.ac.uk
WWW: http://www.dur.ac.uk/-dbr0www/

Eclipse Group Ltd
18-20 Highbury Place
London N5 1QP
UK
Tel: +44 171 354 5858
Fax: +44 171 354 8106
E-mail: julia.gosling@irseclipse.co.uk

Teleworking

EcoPlan International
Centre for Technology & Systems Studies
10 Rue Joseph Bara
F-75006 Paris
France
Tel: +33 1 4326 13 23
Fax: +33 1 43 26 07 46
E-mail: 100336.2154@compuserve.com
WWW: http://www.the-commons.org/

Empirica
Oxfordstraße 2
D-53111 Bonn
Germany
Tel: +49 228 985300
Fax: +49 228 9853012
E-mail: werner@emp-d.uucp or
100065.1675@compuserve.com

European Community Telework/Telematics Forum (ECTF)
12 Castle Street
Totnes
Devon TQ9 5NU
UK
Tel: +44 1803 865 852
Fax: +44 1803 868 377
E-mail: protocol@ectf.org.uk

European Foundation for the Improvement of Living and
Working Conditions
Loughlinstown House
Shankill
Co. Dublin
Ireland
Fax: + 353 1 282 6456

European Telework Online
WWW: http://www.eto.org.uk

Family Policy Studies Centre
231 Baker Street
London NW1 6XE, UK
Tel: +44 171 486 8211
Fax: +44 171 224 3510
E-mail: fpsc@clus1.ulcc.ac.uk

Telework resource list

Natalie Fay
Bay Area Telecommuting Assistance Project
c/o ABAG
PO Box 2050
Oakland, CA 94604-2050
USA
Fax: +1 510 464 7970

Finnish Ministry of Labour
PO Box 30
FIN-00101 Helsinki
Finland
Tel: +358 0 1856906
Fax: +358 0 18569063
WWW: http://www.tkk.utu.fi/telework/

Flexible Working Magazine
Eclipse Group Ltd
18-20 Highbury Place
London N5 1QP
UK
Tel: +44 171 354 5858
Fax: +44 171 354 8106
E-mail: julia.gosling@irseclipse.co.uk

Ted Fuller
Director
Durham University Business School
Knowledge Systems Research Centre
Mill Hill Lane
Durham City DH1 3LB
UK
Tel: +44 191 374 2211
Fax: +44 191 374 3748
E-mail Ted.Fuller@durham.ac.uk
WWW: http://www.dur.ac.uk/-dbr0www/

Gil Gordon Associates
10 Donner Court
Monmouth Junction, NJ 08852
USA
Tel: +1 908 329 2266
Fax: + 1 908 329 2703
E-mail: 74375.1667@compuserve.com

...in brief   Teleworking

Health & Safety Authority
10 Hogan Place
Dublin 2
Ireland
Tel: +353 1 662 0400
Fax: +353 1 662 0417
E-mail: JM@HSA.IE

Legal and Contractual Situation of Teleworkers in Finland
Asko Heikkilä
Ministry of Labour
PO Box 30
FIN-00101 Helsinki
Finland
Tel: +358 0 1856906
Fax: +358 0 18569063
WWW: http://www.tkk.utu.fi/telework/

Work and Family Benefits Provided by Major US
Employers in 1995
Hewitt Associates SA
Avenue des Cerisiers 15, b2
B-1030 Brussels
Belgium
Tel: +32 2 743 86 11
Fax: +32 2 743 86 12

Highlands & Islands Enterprise
Bridge House
20 Bridge Street
Inverness IV1 1QR
UK
Tel: + 44 1463 234171
Fax: + 44 1463 244 469
E-mail HIE_GENERAL@HIENT.CO.UK

Tony Hodgson
IDON
Edradour House
Pitlochry
Perthshire PH16 5JW
UK
Tel: + 44 1796 47 37 73
Fax: + 44 1796 47 37 09
E-mail: tony@idon.demon.co.uk

218

Telework resource list

Noel Hodson
14 Brookside
Headington
Oxford OX3 7PJ
Tel: +44 1865 60994
Fax: +44 1865 64520
E-mail : 100143.2571@compuserve.com

The Home Office Partnership
St John's Innovation Centre
Cowley Road
Cambridge CB4 4WS, UK
Tel: +44 1223 421911
Fax: +44 1223 421760
E-mail: hop@hop.co.uk

Home Run Newsletter
Active Information
Cribau Mill
Llanvair Discoed
Chepstow
Gwent NP6 6RD
UK
Tel: +44 1291 641 222
Fax: +44 1291 641 777
E-mail: 100117.27@compuserve.com

Ursula Huws
Analytica
46 Ferntower Road
London N5 2JH
UK
Tel: +44 171 226 8411
Fax: +44 171 226 0813
E-mail: analytica@dial.pipex.com
WWW: http://dspace.dial.pipex.xom/analytica

IBM
PO Box 41
North Harbour
Portsmouth
Hampshire PO6 3AU
UK
Tel: +44 1705 561000
Fax: +44 1705 210846

Teleworking

IDON
Edradour House
Pitlochry
Perthshire PH16 5JW
UK
Tel: + 44 1796 47 37 73
Fax: + 44 1796 47 37 09
E-mail: tony@idon.demon.co.uk

The Institute of Management Foundation
Management House
Cottingham Road
Corby
Northants NN17 1TT
UK
Tel: +44 1536 204222
Fax: +44 1536 201651
E-mail: savoy@inst-mgt.org.uk

International Teleconferencing Association
Suite 200
1650 Tysons Boulevard
McLean VA 22102
Tel: +1 703 506 3280
Fax: +1 703 506 3266
E-mail: dasitca@aol.com

JALA International Inc.
971 Stonehill Lane
Los Angeles CA 90049
USA
Tel: +1 310 476 3703
Fax: +1 310 476 6007
E-mail: jala@ix.netcom.com or
72155.706@compuserve.com

Telework resource list

Andrew James
Editor
Home Run Newsletter
Active Information
Cribau Mill
Llanvair Discoed
Chepstow
Gwent NP6 6RD
UK
Tel: +44 1291 641 222
Fax: +44 1291 641 777
E-mail: 100117.27@compuserve.com

Chris Jensen-Butler
TeleDanmark Consult
Skanderborgvej 232
PO Box 2245
DK 8260 Viby J
Denmark
Tel: + 45 86 28 64 55
Fax: +45 86 28 64 99
E-mail: 100117.1157@compuserve.com

Peter Johnston
DGXIII-B
Rue de la Loi 200
B-1049 Brussels
Belgium
Tel: +32 2 299 11 11
Fax: +32 2 296 88 80
E-mail: PDG@Postman.dg13.cec.be

Wendell H. Joice PhD
US Office of Personnel Management
Career Entry Group
Office of Personnel Research and Development
1900 E Street, NW
Washington, DC 20415-0001
USA
Tel: +1 202 273 4669
Fax: + 1 202 273 4670
E-mail:Wendell.Joice@gsa.gov

Teleworking

Paul Joyce
Flexible Working Magazine
Eclipse Group Ltd
18-20 Highbury Place
London N5 1QP
UK
Tel: +44 171 354 5858
Fax: +44 171 354 8106
E-mail: paul.joyce@irseclipse.co.uk

Kay Business Services Ltd (KBS)
PO Box 173
Purley
Surrey CR8 4ZY
UK
Tel: +44 181 660 5008
Fax: +44 181 660 5008
E-mail: kbs@mbkay.demon.co.uk
WWW: http://www.demon.co.uk/kbs

Ki Net
Dower House
Lethen
Nairn IV12 5PR
UK
Tel: +44 1667 452123
Fax: +44 1667 452123
E-Mail: ki-net@netinnov.co.uk

Werner Korte
empirica
Oxfordstraße 2
D-53111 Bonn
Germany
Tel: +49 228 985300
Fax: +49 228 9853012
E-mail: werner@emp-d.uucp or
100065.1675@compuserve.com

June Langhoff
E-mail: Jlanghoff@aol.com

Telework resource list

Ari Luukinen
Ministry of Labour
PO Box 30
FIN-00101 Helsinki
Finland
Tel: +358 0 18569061
Fax: +358 0 18569063
E-mail: ari.luukinen@tkk.utu.fi
WWW: http://www.tkk.utu.fi/telework/

Management Technology Associates (MTA)
Clark House
Kings Road
Fleet
Hampshire GU13 9AD, UK
Tel: +44 1252 812252
Fax: +44 1252 815702
E-mail: 100142.31@compuserve.com or info@mtanet.co.uk
WWW: http://www.mtanet.co.uk/

Kurt McDaniel
Chase Plaza Telecommuting Centre
Tel: +1 405 749 9782
Fax: +1 405 749 8516
E-mail: kurt.mcdaniel@gsa.gov

Harry Metz
TeleTeam Holland
Postbus 393
NL-8330 AJ Steenwijk
The Netherlands
Tel: +31 5210 18557
Fax: +31 5210 18991
E-mail 100265.2647@compuserve.com

Jeremy Millard
TeleDanmark Consult
Skanderborgvej 232
PO Box 2245
DK 8260 Viby J
Denmark
Tel: + 45 86 28 64 55
Fax: +45 86 28 64 99
E-mail: 100117.1157@compuserve.com or
jeremy@aix1.danadata.dk

Teleworking

Horace Mitchell
Management Technology Associates (MTA)
Tel: +44 1252 812252
Fax: +44 1252 815702
E-mail: 100136.2412@compuserve.com or
info@mtanet.co.uk
WWW: http://www.mtanet.co.uk/

National Association of Teleworkers (NAT)
Tel: +44 1736 33 27 36

National Rural Enterprise Centre
Stoneleigh Park
Warwickshire
CV8 2RR
Tel: +44 1203 690691
Fax: +44 1203 696 770
E-mail: 100114.2366@compuserve.com

Netherlands Telework Platform (PTN)
PO Box 190
NL-2700 Zoetermeer
The Netherlands
Tel: +31 79 531100
Fax: +31 79 531 365

New Ways To Work
309 Upper Street
London N1 2TY
UK
Tel: +44 171 226 4026
Fax: + 44 171 354 2978

Jack Nilles
JALA International Inc.
971 Stonehill Lane
Los Angeles CA 90049
USA
Tel: +1 310 476 3703
Fax: +1 310 476 6007
E-mail: jala@ix.netcom.com or
72155.706@compuserve.com

Telework resource list

[PATRA]
Professor David Oborne
University of Swansea
Department of Psychology
Science Tower
Singleton Park
Swansea SA2 8PP
UK
Tel: +44 1792 295 606
Fax: +44 1792 295 679
E-mail: d.j.oborne@SWANSEA.AC.UK

Office of Personnel Management (US)
Office of Labour Relations & Workforce Performance
Work & Family Programme Centre
1900 E. Street
OPRD Room 6462
Washington DC 20415
USA

Olsten Corporation
175 Broad Hollow Road
Melvill NY 11747-8905
Fax: + 1 516 844 7022

Oregon Department of Energy
Telecommuting Resources
625 Marion Street NE
Salem
Oregon 97310
USA
Tel: +1 503 378 4040 (In Oregon 1-800-221-8035)
Fax: +1 503 373 7806

Pacific Bell
27392 Camino Capistrano
Room 200
Laguna Higuel CA 92677
USA
Fax: + 1714 248 8339

Teleworking

Andrew Page
Protocol Communications
Tel: +44 1803 865 852
Fax: +44 1803 868 377

Juhani Pekkola
Project Coordinator
Ministry of Labour
National Workplace Development Programme
PO Box 524
FIN-00101 Helsinki
Finland
Tel: +358 0 18568950
Fax: +358 0 18568961
E-mail: juhani.pekkola@pt2.tempo.mol.fi
WWW: http://www.tkk.utu.fi/telework/

Cindy Pothier
TeleTeam USA
PO Box 14678
Boise
Idaho 83711-0678
E-mail: 100265.3347@compuserve.com

Victor A. de Pous
16 Anton Constandsestraat
NL-1098 HX Amsterdam
PO Box 51005
NL-1007 EA Amsterdam
The Netherlands
tel: +31 20 665 5738
Fax: +31 20 665 5818
E-mail: vdepous@nedernet.nl

Christopher A. Pownall
151 Carella Street
Howrah
Tasmania 7018
Australia
Tel: +61 2 47 7920
E-mail: cpownall@postoffice.utas.edu.au

Telework resource list

Jenny Procter
AT&T
1945 Chaussée de Wavre
B-1160 Brussels
Belgium
Tel: +32 2 676 35 90
Fax: +32 2 676 35 04

Protocol Communications
Tel: +44 1803 865 852
Fax: +44 1803 868 377

Proto-Type
Spinney House
Compasses Road
Pattiswick
Essex CM7 8BG
UK
Tel: +44 1376 561 010
Fax: +44 1376 562 899
E-mail: 101665.405@compuserve.com

Puget Sound Telecommuting Demonstration
Washington State Energy Office
925 Plum St SE
Bldg 4
PO Box 43165
Olympia WA 98504-3165
USA
Tel: +1 360 956 2055
Fax: +1 360 956 2218

Remote Electronic Construction Industry Telematics
Experiment (RECITE)
Commission of the European Communities
Directorate General XIII
200 Rue de la Loi
B-1049 Brussels
Tel: +32 2 299 11 11
Fax: +32 2 296 24 75

...in brief

Teleworking

Scottish Teleworking Association (STA)
19 Bellfield Road
North Kessock
Inverness IV1 1XU
Scotland
UK
Tel: +44 1463 731888
Fax: + 44 1463 731 524
E-mail: 100031.1511@compuserve.com

David J. Skyrme
David Skyrme Associates Ltd
Newbury
Berkshire
UK
Tel: +44 1635 551434
Fax: +44 1635 551434
E-mail: david@pop3.hiway.co.uk
WWW: http://www.hiway.co.uk/skyrme/index.htm

Smart Valley Inc.
2520 Mission College
Santa Clara CA 95054
USA
Tel: +1 408 562 7795
Fax: +1 408 562 7677
E-mail: kathieb@svi.org

Systems Synthesis Ltd
Waterloo House
Waterloo Street
Clifton
Bristol BS8 4BT
UK
Tel: +44 117 923 8853
Fax: +44 117 923 88 34
E-mail: info@ssynth.demon.co.uk

Telework resource list

Dr Grant Tate
Bridgewater Research Group NL
Aalbekerweg 67d
NL-6336 XN Hulsberg
The Netherlands
Tel: +31 45 405 2865
Fax: +31 45 405 9245
E-mail: 72261.526@compuserve.com

Telecommute America!
PO Box 9536
Scottsdale
Arizona 85252-9536
USA

Telecommuting Review Newsletter
Gil Gordon Associates
10 Donner Court
Monmouth Junction, NJ 08852
USA
Tel: +1 908 329 2266
Fax: + 1 908 329 2703
E-mail: 74375.1667@compuserve.com

The Telecottage Association
Wren Telecottage
Stoneleigh Park
Warwickshire CV8 2RR
UK
Tel: +44 1203 696 986
Fax: +44 1203 696 538
E-mail: 100114.2366@compuserve.com

TeleDanmark Consult
Skanderborgvej 232
PO Box 2245
DK 8260 Viby J
Denmark
Tel: +45 86 28 64 55
Fax: +45 86 28 64 99
E-mail: 100117.1157@compuserve.com

Teleworking

Telenor Research
PO Box 83
N-2007 Kjeller
Norway
Tel: +47 63 80 91 00
Fax: + 47 6381 0076
E-mail : john.bakke@fou.telenor.no

TeleTeam Holland
Postbus 393
NL-8330 AJ Steenwijk
The Netherlands
Tel: +31 5210 18557
Fax: +31 5210 18991
E-mail 100265.2647@compuserve.com

TeleTeam UK.
17 Shannon Close
Grove OX12 7PT
UK
Tel: +44 831 332888 or +44 589 083842
Fax: +44 1235 766568
E-mail: 100112.323@compuserve.com

TeleTeam USA
PO Box 14678
Boise
Idaho 83711-0678
USA
Tel: +1 412 421 4479 (voice mail)
Fax: + 1 412 421 2670
E-mail: 100265.3347@compuserve.com

Teleworker Magazine
The Other Cottage
Shortwood
Nailsworth
Gloucestershire GL6 0SH
UK
Tel: +44 1453 834 874
Fax: +44 1453 836 174
E-mail: 100272.3137@compuserve.com

Telework resource list

US General Services Administration
Office of Work Place Initiatives
Washington DC 20405
USA

Christina Van Wanseele
Caltrans – Right of Way
PO Box 85406
San Diego CA 92106
Tel: +1 619 688 6907
E-mail: CVanWans@TRMX3.DOT.CA.GOV

Warwickshire Rural Enterprise Network (WREN)
Telecottage
Stoneleigh Park
Warwickshire CV8 2RR
UK
Tel: +441203 696 986
Fax: +44 1203 696538
E-mail: 100114.2366@compuserve.com or
WREN@midnet.com

Washington State Energy Office
925 Plum St SE
Bldg 4
PO Box 43165
Olympia WA 98504-3165
USA
Tel: +1 206 956 2000
Fax: +1 206 956 2217

Peter Wingrave
Design & Construction Manager
Property Department
IBM
PO Box 41
North Harbour
Portsmouth
Hampshire PO6 3AU
UK
Tel: +44 1705 568680
Fax: +44 1705 210846
E-mail: peter_wingrave@OK.IBM.COM

Teleworking

Michael Wolff
Ki Net
Dower House
Lethen
Nairn IV12 5PR
UK
Tel: +44 1667 452123
Fax: +44 1667 452123
E-Mail: ki-net@netinnov.co.uk or
100424.440@compuserve.com

Working from Home Forum
Compuserve
[GO WORK]

World Future Society
7910 Woodmont Avenue
Suite 450
Bethesda
Maryland 20814
USA
Tel: +1 301 656 8274
Fax: +1 301 951 0394

WREN Business Services
WREN Telecottage
Stoneleigh Park
Warwickshire CV8 2RR
UK
Tel: +441203 696 986
Fax: +44 1203 696538
E-mail: 100114.2366@compuserve.com or
WREN@midnet.com

Thomas E. Youngs, Jr
TeleTeam USA
PO Box 14678
Boise
Idaho 83711-0678
USA
Tel: +1 412 421 4479 (voice mail)
Fax: + 1 412 421 2670
E-mail: 100265.3347@compuserve.com

Telework resource list

Marya Zaminder
Researcher
Ministry of Labour
PO Box 30
FIN-00101 Helsinki
Finland
Tel: +358 0 18569066
Fax: +358 0 18569063
WWW: http://www.tkk.utu.fi/telework/

15 References

Bibby, Andrew, Teleworking Thirteen Journeys to the Future of Work, Calouste Gulbenkian Foundation, 1995

Bjerklie, David, 'Telecommuting preparing for round two (challenges and benefits to employers)', Technology Review, **98**, No. 5, 20 (2), July 1995

Blair, Laura, 'Enter the masters of time and space,' Facilities Management Supplement, The Times, 22 March, 1996

Burch, Steven, Teleworking: A Strategic Guide for Management, Kogan Page, 1991

DeMarco, Anthony, The Dawning of the Telecommuter Age, Facilties Design & Management, April 1995

Gray, M., Hodson, N. and Gordon, G., Teleworking Explained, John Wiley, 1993

Hannon, Kerry, 'A long way from the rat race: the charms of Telluride have made a telecommuting town', US News & World Report, **119**, No.17, 86 (2), October 1995

Irving, R. and Tivey, J., Management Directions: Flexible Working Practices and Homeworking, The Institute of Management Foundation, 1995

Kinsmann, Francis, The Telecommuters, John Wiley 1987

Langhoff, June, Telecom Made Easy, Aegis Publishing group, Newport, 1995

Murphy, Edna, in association with the Institute of Directors, Flexible Work, Director Books, 1996

Nilles, Jack M., Making Telecommuting Happen: A Guide for Telemanagers and Telecommuters, Van Nostrand Reinhold, 1994

References

Rao, Srikumar S., 'The multi-armed corporation,' Financial World, **164**, No.12, 76(2), May 1995

Schepp, D. and Schepp, B., The Telecommuter's Handbook: How to Earn a Living Without Going to the Office, McGraw-Hill, 1995

Skyrme, David J., 'Take a look at Teleworking', Management Consultancy, June 1994

Thomas, Irene Middleman, 'No more 9 to 5', Hispanic, **8**, No. 6, 68(2), July 1995

Verespej, Michael A., 'Virtually officeless: Dick Grove wanted to go back home, so he let his employees do the same', Industry Week, **244**, No. 17, 55(1), September 1995

Woods, M., Whitehead, J. and Lamplugh, D., Working Alone, Surviving and Thriving, Pitman Publishing, 1993

Index

Index

For Product Safety Concerns and Information please contact our EU representative GPSR@taylorandfrancis.com Taylor & Francis Verlag GmbH, Kaufingerstraße 24, 80331 München, Germany

T - #0104 - 160425 - C0 - 234/156/14 - PB - 9780750628754 - Gloss Lamination